Growing Up in God's Word

Bible Curriculum

"... from childhood you have known the Holy Scriptures..."
(II Timothy 3:15, NKJV)

LIFE OF CHRIST
Part 1

Table of Contents

Introduction..5

How to Use this Curriculum...6

Suggested Schedule 8

A Word About the Gospels...9

Lesson 1: Angels Announce the Birth of Jesus...10

Lesson 2: The Birth of Jesus...15

Lesson 3: Visit of the Wise Men and the Flight to Egypt...............................20

Lesson 4: Jesus' Childhood...26

Lesson 5: Baptism of Jesus...32

Lesson 6: Temptation of Jesus..38

Lesson 7: Jesus Calls Disciples 43

Lesson 8: Jesus' First Miracle...49

Lesson 9: Jesus and the Woman at the Well..54

Lesson 10: The Sermon on the Mount...60

Lesson 11: Jesus Heals a Paralytic..69

Lesson 12: Jesus Calms the Storm..75

Lesson 13: Feeding the Five Thousand and Jesus Walks on the Water 81

ANSWER KEY 89

Appendix A – Maps 104

Map 1 – Palestine...105

Map 2 – Egypt, Palestine, Mesopotamia...106

Map 3 – Sea of Galilee 107

Map 4 – Middle East, Far East, Africa 108

Appendix B – Templates 109

Introduction

Why teach children the Bible using only the Bible? Can they understand it? Yes! Is it too boring? No! I have taught a children's Bible class on Sunday mornings for over twenty years and have home-schooled my three children, teaching them the Bible in our home. Guess what? Children are a lot smarter than we give them credit for! There are just a few key things to remember in teaching the Bible to children. First, we need to be enthusiastic about the Bible ourselves. If children see that we think the Bible is boring, they will most likely adopt the same opinion. Be excited about opening the word of God together! Second, don't be afraid to tell them you don't know know an answer to their question. There are many things in the Bible that we have questions about; some things we are able to study and find an answer for, others will have to wait until we get to heaven and can ask God. It's okay to let them know you're stumped too, but encourage them to search for the answer with you. Third, set the bar high for them. Please, please, please don't "dumb" the Bible down to "their level". Children can understand a lot through patient explanation and teaching. For example, if you read a hard word in the Bible that they may not be familiar with, stop and ask them what they think it means, then give them a correct definition. Now they have learned a new word and understand the passage you've just read at the same time. Children like to be challenged and to meet our expectations for them.

The method in this curriculum works because it has been tried among many children of different ages, abilities and levels. Here is the best proof I can offer to you: One of my regular Sunday morning students brought a friend to our class one day. She answered a few questions but mostly sat very quietly, absorbing everything that was going on. Later on, the woman that brought her to church said that the little girl told her on the way home that she wanted to come to our Sunday school class every week because we *actually teach from the Bible.* This little girl is not "unchurched" by any means; in fact, she regularly attends a denominational megachurch every Sunday. As the scripture says, "Out of the mouths of babes!"

May your children be like Timothy in the Bible who, *"from childhood has known the holy Scriptures"* (II Timothy 3:15) and may God bless you as you study His word together.

How to Use this Curriculum

Life began in a garden, so we will be using garden references and symbols throughout this curriculum to designate the different activities. Luke 8:11 says that *"the seed is the word of God"*. Our hearts are the soil that the seed needs to be planted in. We should desire to cultivate the soil of our hearts and the hearts of our children to receive the word so that it will grow and produce good fruit for our Lord.

"Growing In The Word": Lesson Text And Discussion

This is the most important part of the curriculum – the teaching of God's Word. The lesson text is broken down into manageable sections to be read aloud and then discussed. If children are old enough to read, let them read out loud. If there are several verses to be read as a section, you could take turns reading a couple of verses per person. If it helps your child, let them jot down notes or write down definitions to new words as you discuss the passage. Encourage them to ask questions and ask them leading questions to get them thinking. The discussion section is basically a paraphrasing of what was just read to make sure there is comprehension of the material. Frequently there are questions to be answered during the discussion phase as well. The section of verses often leave off at a "cliffhanger" moment which helps keep the children engaged. You read and discuss and then you're ready to read on to see what happens next. At the end of this section of the curriculum there are review questions. These can be used in several ways: You may ask them at the end of the lesson, at the end of the week for a review, or if you want to have a graded assignment, you can use them as an oral or written quiz.

*A word about translations. It is important to use a reliable and accurate translation. Some dependable ones are KJV, NKJV, and ASV (American Standard). Many modern translations have compromised the integrity of the Scriptures in trying to put it in "easier to understand" language. All references in this curriculum are taken from the New King James Version.

"Putting Down Roots": Memory Work

Memory work should be practiced every day for the entire week. Use whatever method works the best according to your child's learning style. (Flashcards, audio recording, repetition, etc.) Here is a link containing a list of aids for memorizing scripture: http://pryorconvictions.com/memorizing-scripture/ The Psalmist said in Psalm 119:11, *"Thy word have I hid in my heart that I might not sin against Thee."* I cannot stress enough how important it is to memorize Scripture. In addition to Scripture, sometimes there are other items included in the Memory Work. A challenge to parents: memorize it with your children!

"Farther Afield": Map Work

There are blank maps provided in Appendix A in the back of the book. These may be photocopied for home use with this curriculum. Most lessons have mapping activities to serve as a visual aid of the places you read about in scripture. To be consistent, you may want to follow a system such as: cities – red, countries – green, bodies of water – blue, wilderness or desert areas – brown, lands or regions – yellow. The map work will indicate different places to be located on the map. Locate and label each item.

"Harvest Fun": Games And Activities

There are games and activities for each lesson to help review and reinforce the material that was covered. It is best to read through these at the beginning of the week to see if any planning ahead needs to be done.

"Digging Deeper": Research

This is primarily for the older students who are able to work independently. If your younger children wish to do these assignments with your help, then by all means, let them! It is a good idea to keep a notebook for these written assignments. These assignments are meant to encourage students of the Bible to learn how to study a topic deeper by using other resources to shed light on the subject. Primarily, books and the Internet will be your sources of information so it's important to do two things: 1) Check the reliability of your source, and 2) Check multiple sources; you might find two or more very different theories or opinions. Some good resources to use are Bible commentaries, concordances (such as Strong's), Bible dictionaries, Bible atlases and Bible software. There are many things we run across in the Bible that we would like to know more about. Have fun exploring!

"Food For Thought": Puzzles

There are at least two puzzles with each lesson to, again, provide review and reinforcement or plain just to have fun! The puzzles may be worked in the book or photocopied. All puzzle answers are provided in the Answer Key in the back of the book.

"Fruits Of Our Labor": Crafts

There are at least two crafts to do with each lesson. They vary in level of difficulty, but are another means of reinforcement of material covered. Crafts are a good activity for the kinesthetic (hands-on) learner as well as a tangible reminder for the visual learner. Please read ahead early in the week to see what materials you may need to gather in advance.

Suggested Schedule

This curriculum is designed to be used five days a week, 30 minutes to 1 hour per day. It is designed to be used with multiple ages with some activities geared toward older children and others geared toward younger. You may use as much or as little of the activities listed as you choose. Please feel free to alter the suggested schedule to fit the time constraints and needs of your family. However, the lesson and memory work portions should be used for all ages.

Begin or end each day's activities with prayer.

- Day 1 – Read "Growing in the Word": Lesson Text and Discussion. Begin "Putting Down Roots": Memory Work assignments.

- Day 2 – Continue memory work, do "Farther Afield": Map Work activities, and "Harvest Fun": Games and Activities.

- Day 3 – Continue memory work, do "Digging Deeper": Research activities, and/or "Food for Thought": Puzzles.

- Day 4 – Continue memory work, do "Fruits of Our Labor": Crafts, or continue working on previous activities.

- Day 5 – Recite memory work, do lesson Review Questions and finish any assignments or activities from the week that time didn't permit.

A Word About the Gospels

In studying the life of Christ, we will be looking at passages from all four gospels: Matthew, Mark, Luke and John. It is important to understand why each of these gospels was written. They were addressed to different people for different purposes.

Matthew was written to the Jews by a Jew and about a Jew. This is why he begins his book with genealogies – something the Jews had great interest in. Mark addresses his gospel to Gentile readers (all non-Jews) who would not be very familiar with Old Testament law. He focuses on the servanthood of Christ. Luke was a physician who writes his account to Theophilus who was possibly a government official or member of nobility. Luke writes from a historical perspective and may have been trying to make the case that Christianity was not a threat to the Roman empire. The gospel of John was written by the apostle John in the Greek language and emphasizes the deity of Jesus.

Taken all together, the gospels paint a complete picture of the birth, life and death of our Lord and Savior, Jesus Christ.

Lesson 1: Angels Announce the Birth of Jesus

Text: Matthew 1:18-25; Luke 1:26-38

"Growing In The Word": Lesson Text And Discussion

Read Matthew 1:18-20. Joseph and Mary were to be married. They were betrothed which is similar to an engagement, but much more committed. A betrothal usually consisted of two families entering into a contract to marry one family's son with the other family's daughter and a dowry, or bride price, was usually involved. If you were betrothed, there was no backing out! You were as good as married; that's why Joseph considers "putting Mary away" or divorcing her when he thought she had been unfaithful to him. A divorce was what would have been necessary to break the betrothal. Now, he loves Mary, but all he knows is she's going to have a baby and he isn't the father! The angel reassures him that it is a very special baby – one from heaven itself through the Holy Spirit. The angel is not named but appears to Joseph to give him instructions. How does the angel appear to Joseph? (In a dream)

Read Matthew 1:21-25. Joseph is told that Mary will have a son to be called Jesus and He will do a wonderful thing – save His people from their sins! It's important to know that everything that happens concerning the birth, life, and death of Jesus is a fulfillment of prophecy; none of it is a coincidence or "just happened". It was all in God's divine plan. The angel quotes an Old Testament prophet to Joseph. Can you guess which one? (Isaiah) Another name for Jesus will be Immanuel. What does that name mean? (God with us) When Joseph awakens he does as commanded and takes Mary for his wife.

Read Luke 1:26-27. This angel is named: Gabriel. He appears to Mary in the city of Nazareth in the region of Galilee. Who sent Gabriel to Mary? (God) Mary is a virgin; she is a pure, unmarried woman. She is betrothed to Joseph.

Read Luke 1:28-29. He greets her by saying she's highly favored and blessed. Mary is clearly puzzled by all of this. What would you think if an angel appeared and greeted you like this? The fact that God chose Mary from all other women to be the mother of Jesus says a lot about the kind of woman she was. What must she have been like to have been chosen by God for such a special task – to be the mother of the Messiah?

Read Luke 1:30-33. Wow! She's told she is going to have a baby boy who will be great, a King, and have a kingdom that lasts forever. Now Mary is just a poor woman, and not yet married to Joseph. Can you imagine what she's thinking? She probably has <u>a lot</u> of questions!

Read Luke 1:34-38. The angel Gabriel now tells her that this baby will be the very Son of God! This is <u>the</u> Messiah that the Jews have watched and waited for for so long. How exciting! Did Mary understand exactly how all of this was going to happen? (No) Mary is also told that her relative, Elizabeth, is six months pregnant (another miracle, since she was old and childless). Do you know who Elizabeth's baby was? (John the Baptist) The angel Gabriel finally tells the astonished Mary that *nothing* is impossible with God. He can do anything! Mary then concludes by saying she's the Lord's servant and she's willing to do whatever He asks of her. Mary trusted God. We need to learn a lesson from Mary – how to be a *willing* servant of the Lord no matter how difficult something is or when we don't understand all of the "why's". Being a cheerful, obedient child of God should always be our goal.

<u>Review Questions</u>: (Answers are in the Answer Key.)

1. Who told Joseph about Jesus' birth? *Angell*

2. How did he appear to Joseph? *in a dream*

3. What did the angel tell Joseph to not be afraid to do? *To marry Mary*

4. What Old Testament prophet is quoted in Matthew 1:23? *Isaiah*

5. What does Immanuel mean? *God with us*

6. What did the angel tell Joseph that Jesus would do? *Save his people from their sins*

7. Who told Mary about Jesus' birth? *Gabriel*

8. What city did Mary live in? *Nazareth*

9. What is impossible with God? *Nothing – all things are possible*

10. Who was Mary's cousin? *Elizabeth*

11. What amazing news did the angel give Mary concerning her cousin? *She would have a child*

12. Mary called herself the __*handmaid*__ of the Lord. *servant*

"Putting Down Roots": Memory Work

- Memorize Matthew 1:23
- Memorize Matthew Luke 1:37

"Farther Afield": Map Work

Map 1

- Locate the city of Nazareth
- Locate the region of Galilee

"Harvest Fun": Games And Activities

- Act it out - Act out the scene where the angel Gabriel announces Jesus' birth to Mary. Dress the parts and be dramatic. Don't forget how the angel greets her: "Rejoice highly favored one!" You may even want to video your scene.

- Deliver the Message - The angels in our lesson were acting as messengers from the Lord. You're going to deliver a message to people in your family. First, make up a message (for example: "I love you", "Have a great day", or "We're having chicken for dinner!"). Second, make up a way to communicate or deliver the message. You could speak it in a foreign language, write in in code, play charades, or write it down and hide it in the house playing "hot or cold" to find it or giving clues to its location.

 ## "Digging Deeper": Research

- The angel Gabriel – This is not the only occasion that we read about Gabriel. See if you can find the other places he's mentioned in the Bible and whom he spoke to.

- Names of Jesus – An angel tells Joseph that Jesus will be called Immanuel meaning "God with us". The Scriptures are full of many names referring to Jesus. How many can you find? Here's just a few to get you started: Counselor (Isaiah 9:6), Lamb of God (John 1:36), The Way (John 14:6)

- Betrothals – Learn what you can about betrothal arrangements in Bible times. Do you think you would have liked to be in a betrothal arrangement? Why or why not?

 ## "Food For Thought": Puzzles

- Crossword Puzzle – The following page contains a crossword puzzle for this lesson. If an answer has more than one word, the space(s) are included. Answers are in the Answer Key.

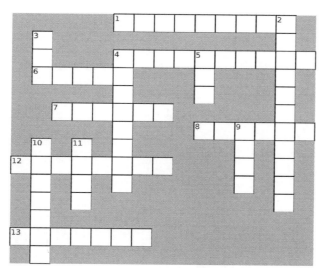

Across

1 Mary's relative who was also pregnant
4 "With God nothing is _____"
6 an angel came to Joseph in a _____
7 Gabriel told Mary not to be _____
8 Mary's betrothed
12 city where Mary lived
13 Mary calls herself the _____ of the Lord

Down

2 Mary was with child of the _____
3 Who sent the angel to Mary?
4 _____ means "God with us"
5 Mary was told her baby would be the _____ of God
9 Joseph was told that Mary's son would save his people from their _____
10 name of angel who visited Mary
11 mother of Jesus

• Coded Message -

| 7 | 19 | 22 | 2 | | 8 | 19 | 26 | 15 | 15 | | 24 | 26 | 15 | 15 | | 19 | 18 | 8 |

| 13 | 26 | 14 | 22 | | 18 | 14 | 14 | 26 | 13 | 6 | 22 | 15 | | 4 | 19 | 18 | 24 | 19 |

___ ___ ___ ___ ___   ___ ___ ___   ___ ___ ___ ___   ___ ___ .

14 22 26 13 8   20 12 23   4 18 7 19   6 8

Key to the Code:

F	N	R	U	A	G	O	S	V	C	H	T	D	I	E	B	W	K	Y	P	M	L	J
21	13	9	6	26	20	12	8	5	24	19	7	23	18	22	25	4	16	2	11	14	15	17

 ## "Fruits Of Our Labor": Crafts

- Make a name for yourself – Angels told Joseph and Mary some different names their child would be called: Jesus, Son of God, Son of the Highest and Immanuel which means "God with us." Find out what your name means and make a name plaque for your room. You will need a rectangular piece of thin wood or poster board or card stock measuring about 5 inches wide by 10 inches long. If you're using wood, you may want to paint a background color first. Write or paint your name in large letters. Underneath it in smaller letters, write or paint the meaning of your name. Decorate your name plaque however you'd like and hang it in your room.

- Make an angel – You will need: Two large white coffee filters, a piece of thin ribbon, gold spray paint, a white twisty tie and glue. (You can substitute acrylic paint with a sponge brush instead of spray paint.) First, make a small ball for the head by rolling up some paper tissue (like kleenex or toilet paper). Place the ball in the middle of one of the coffee filters then pull the filter up around the ball. Tie the piece of ribbon around the filter over the ball. Turn it upside down with the covered ball now as the head of the angel and the rest of the filter as its gown. Tie the ribbon in a bow at the neck. If you'd like, draw a face on the angel with a marker very carefully. For the wings: Take the other coffee filter and lightly spray gold paint on both sides. Let it dry. Fold the coffee filter in half, then pinch it together in the middle to form wings. Wrap a white twisty tie around the pinched portion to keep it in place. Glue the wings to the back of the angel at the neck and upper back.

Lesson 2: The Birth of Jesus

Text: Luke 2:1-20

"Growing In The Word": Lesson Text And Discussion

Read Luke 2:1-5. Caesar Augustus was the ruler of the Roman empire which was in power at the time of Jesus' birth. He ordered (decreed) that a census be taken. In other words, he wanted a head count of every citizen in his empire. In order to be counted, everyone had to travel to the city of their family home. Joseph and Mary both lived in Nazareth, but had to travel to Bethlehem to register. Bethlehem was also known by another name. What is it? (City of David) The distance from Nazareth to Bethlehem was about 80 miles and Mary was <u>very</u> pregnant. It would probably have taken anywhere from four days to a week for them to travel this distance.

Read Luke 2:6-7. We don't know how long they were in Bethlehem before it was time for Jesus' birth, but whatever the case, the city was probably crowded with travelers like themselves and there was no room in the inn. Mary was forced to give birth in a place where animals were kept, such as a stable. In it was a feeding trough, or manger, which she used as a bed to lay her newborn in. What was Jesus wrapped in? (Swaddling cloths) When Jewish babies were born, they were wrapped up tightly like little mummies in cloth made from linen or cotton. This is what it means to "swaddle" the baby.

Read Luke 2:8-14. It's interesting to see who the angel announces Jesus' birth to - shepherds who were poor, humble men instead of to people such as kings or princes or the rich and powerful. What time of day is it? (Night) What was the shepherds' reaction when the angel first appears? (They were greatly afraid.) The angel tells them not to be afraid because he has some great news for them. A Savior is born! Who did the angel say the good tidings of great joy would be for? (All people) The shepherds are told where to find the newborn King, how he'd be wrapped in swaddling cloths, and lying in a manger. Then a host of angels appeared and what did they do? (They praised God for this wonderful event!)

Read Luke 2:15-20. If you were one of the shepherds, how would you feel after what you'd just seen and heard? They were excited at this incredible news! They hurried into the city to find the baby Jesus. They found Mary, Joseph, and the babe just as they were told. Then they did what anyone with good news does – told someone else! They spread the good news far and wide. Do you share good news when you have it? You have the good news of Jesus Christ! Share it with everyone you meet!

Review Questions: (Answers are in the Answer Key.)

1. Which Caesar ordered a census be taken?

2. What city did Joseph and Mary live in?

3. What city did they have to travel to?

4. What did Mary wrap baby Jesus in?

5. What did Mary lay Jesus in?

6. Who were out in the fields at night?

7. Who appeared to them?

8. What was the message he gave to the shepherds?

9. After the shepherds visited Mary, Joseph, and baby Jesus, what did they do?

10. Whom did they glorify and praise for what they had seen and heard?

 ## "Putting Down Roots": Memory Work

- Memorize Luke 2:10, 11
- Memorize Luke 2:14

 ## "Farther Afield": Map Work

Map 1

- Locate the city of Bethlehem
- Locate the region of Judea

 ## "Harvest Fun": Games And Activities

- Charades – Write down the following characters from this lesson on slips of paper, then take turns drawing a slip of paper and acting it out for everyone else to guess. Characters: Caesar Augustus, Mary, shepherd, Joseph, innkeeper, angel of the Lord (messenger), angel (praising God), baby Jesus, and if you really want to have fun...a sheep!

"Digging Deeper": Research

- Genealogy of Jesus – Trace Jesus' lineage through Joseph (Matthew 1:1-17) and then through Mary (Luke 3:23-38). It may help you to make a chart with two columns in order to make comparisons. In Luke 3:23 when it says, "Joseph, son of Heli" this is referring to Joseph's father-in-law, Mary's father. Notice in Matthew 1:16 who the father of Joseph is. Do both genealogies go back to King David? What are the similarities in the genealogies and at what point do the differences begin?

- Swaddling Cloths – Read about the process of washing and swaddling the babies after birth. Are there any scriptures that talk about this process?

- Christmas – Many Christians celebrate the birth of Jesus on December 25. Does the Bible actually say that's when He was born? Sometimes it's hard to separate fact from fiction when we've grown so used to an idea or seen it portrayed in pictures, etc. If we want to know the truth, we can turn to the Bible. When the Bible doesn't give us information about something, we're not at liberty to "fill in the details". Revelation 22:18, 19 makes it clear that we are not to add to or take away from the word of God. So, what *is* the truth about Christmas and how it relates to the birth of Jesus? Research the origin of Christmas and some of the traditions associated with it, and also some of the myths about it. Who designated December 25th as Christmas day? Were the wise men present at Jesus' birth as shown in nativity scenes? What time of year would the shepherds have their flocks out at night? Write down and share what you learn. Be willing to keep an open mind. Remember – the Bible is our source for truth.

"Food For Thought": Puzzles

- Who Am I/What Am I? - Read each clue and guess the answer. Answers are in the Answer Key.

1. Another name for me is a feeding trough. _____

2. I am a ruler and ordered all the world to be counted and taxed. _____

3. I visited the baby Jesus at his birth. _____

4. I was in the field and heard the angels sing, but couldn't join in. _____

5. I am from Nazareth and listened carefully and quietly to what was said by the visitors about my baby. _____

6. I am from Nazareth and traveled to Bethlehem to be registered along with my wife. _____

7. I am a place where visitors stay. _____

8. My other name is the city of David. _____

9. I'm not paper, but am used for wrapping. _____

10. I am the hometown of Jesus' parents. _____

• Word Search Puzzle – Answers are in the Answer Key.

```
O D M E H E L H T E B Y J E F
N A E S E F N A C E N S U S L
J E E B M H I I J R C U D L O
S N A A P F N E S C A S E E C
W B R E G N A M L E E E A G K
Y Y S H E P H E R D S J M N S
G O E W G N I L D D A W S A P
J C S S N R R G L O R Y S L E
```

decree	Caesar	census	Bethlehem
Judea	Joseph	Mary	manger
inn	shepherds	flock	field
angels	baby	Jesus	swaddling
glory	news		

 **"Fruit Of Our Labor": Crafts**

- Baby Jesus in a manger – Take a wooden clothespin with a solid round head and draw a sleeping face on it with a Sharpie. Take a small strip of soft fabric (like flannel) and wrap up the body of the clothespin. Secure it with a few dots of glue. Using play-doh or modeling clay, make a manger. It will be a long rectangular box open on top and with small legs under it. Lay baby Jesus in his manger. You may want to add some pieces of hay or straw to cushion him.

- Diorama – A diorama is a scene in miniature. Make a diorama of the scene of the shepherds in the field with their sheep and the angel appearing to them. Start with a large shoe box turned on its side for your scene. Add greenery, hills, "water", the sheep, the shepherds and the angel suspended above them. Remember, it's at night so you'll need a black sky with stars. You can be very creative with this. You can use paints, markers, stickers, clay figures, store bought figures, pipe cleaners, etc. Use your imagination! There are some good resources online to give you directions and tips on making dioramas and different effects for your scenery such as realistic-looking water.

Lesson 3: Visit of the Wise Men and the Flight to Egypt

Text: Matthew 2:1-23

"Growing In The Word": Lesson Text And Discussion

Read Matthew 2:1-2. How many wise men came to see Jesus? We don't know for certain because the Bible doesn't tell us. It is generally believed there were three simply because there were three gifts given to the baby Jesus, but the truth is we just don't know. They came from "the East", either the Middle East or the Far East. It's been speculated that they might have come from Persia, Arabia, Babylon, or even India but again, we're not told specifically. One thing these wise men were known for was their skill in Astronomy. They studied the stars, so when they saw this "star", they knew it was significant, and traveled far to find the young king in order to worship him.

Read Matthew 2:3-8. At this time, Herod is king over the land of Judea. He rules over the Jews as a king, but he is subject to the Roman empire. He pushes the panic button when the wise men come to Jerusalem looking for the newborn "king of the Jews". That's his title! (So he thinks.) The wise men arrive in Jerusalem and ask Herod where this new king is to be born. Herod asks the Jewish chief priests and scribes and they tell him Bethlehem. Herod then tells the wise men he wants to find him so he can worship him too, but he's lying. He wants to kill Jesus so that he (Herod) can remain king.

Read Matthew 2:9-12. When the wise men see the star settle over the house where Jesus is, notice their reaction – they rejoiced with "exceeding great joy" to have found Jesus. We should have the same great joy when we recognize Jesus as our king and then desire to worship Him! Notice that Jesus was not in the manger anymore. He is now in a house in Bethlehem where his family is currently living. In our last lesson, in the book of Luke, when the shepherds came to see Jesus the Bible referred to him as "the babe". In Matthew 2:11 when the wise men came to see him, how is he referred to? (As "the young child") The wise men would have traveled a long way to find Jesus, perhaps a journey of several months, so Jesus was more than likely at least a few months old or even over a year old at this time. The gifts they gave him were very valuable and probably helped Mary and Joseph with expenses especially when they went to live in Egypt for awhile. What were the three gifts? (Gold, frankincense, and myrrh) The wise men don't intend to deceive King Herod by not returning to him to tell him where Jesus is, but rather they've been warned by God not to go back to him but to go home in another direction. How did God warn them? (In a dream) They obey <u>God</u>, not the king.

Read Matthew 2:13-15. Joseph is also warned in a dream that King Herod wants to destroy little Jesus. What country does Joseph take his family to? (Egypt) The family flees to the land of Egypt just as it was prophesied. The Old Testament prophet, Hosea, wrote in Hosea 11:1, *"Out of Egypt I called My Son"*. Joseph, Mary and Jesus stay in Egypt until the death of Herod.

Read Matthew 2:16-18. Herod is very angry that the wise men don't return to give him his much-wanted information. He thinks he is being tricked! In his anger, he issues a terrible order: to kill all the baby boys aged two and under in Bethlehem and the surrounding districts. Why aged two and under? He is trying to determine how old Jesus might be according to the timing of the visit of the wise men. He is determined to destroy him. What an evil man!

Read Matthew 2:19-23. A short time later, King Herod dies and Joseph is again told in a dream that it is safe to return home. They settle in the city of Nazareth in the region of Galilee. Herod's son is now ruling in Judea so they don't want to live in that region. What was it prophesied that Jesus was to be called? (He would be called a Nazarene, meaning he's from Nazareth.) It's important to note that *every* prophecy concerning Jesus was fulfilled (came true)!

*An interesting resource for this lesson is a DVD entitled "The Star of Bethlehem." An attorney, who became an amateur astronomer, shares some amazing findings regarding the star which certainly gives one food for thought. It is documentary style and geared to older children, teens, and adults.

Review Questions: (Answers are in the Answer Key.)

1. In what city was Jesus born?
2. Who was king of Judea?
3. Where did the wise men come from?
4. How many wise men were there?
5. Why did Herod want to find Jesus?
6. Why did the wise men want to find him?
7. What led the wise men to Jesus?
8. What gifts did they give Jesus?
9. How were the wise men warned not to return to Herod?
10. Where was Joseph told to take Mary and Jesus?
11. What Old Testament prophet prophesied that Jesus would be in Egypt?
12. When was Joseph told it was safe to return from Egypt?
13. Where did Jesus' family go to live?
14. What wicked order did Herod issue?

"Putting Down Roots": Memory Work

- Memorize Matthew 2:11
- Memorize Hosea 11:1b

 ## "Farther Afield": Map Work

Maps 2 & 4

- Locate the country of Egypt
- Locate some of the possible countries of origin of the wise men: Persia, Babylon, India – whatever country in the East they came from, this shows you the great distance they would have traveled to get to Israel.

 ## "Harvest Fun": Games And Activities

- Hide from Herod! - King Herod did <u>not</u> want to celebrate Jesus' birth because he thought Jesus was to be an earthly king of the Jews who would replace him. He tried to find and destroy the baby Jesus but did not succeed. As God instructed Joseph, he fled with his family to Egypt, hiding Jesus far away from Herod. Let one person be "it"; that person is King Herod. Everyone else has to run and hide from him while he counts to 20. See if everyone can remain successfully hidden from Herod!

- Follow the star – You will need a package of plastic stars or star stickers and a small baby doll. Without letting the kids see, hide stars in different locations around the house. For example, the microwave oven, in the bathtub, under a pillow, on a dining room chair, etc. Take a small baby doll to represent baby Jesus and hide him as well. Make clues to lead the children from location to location, collecting the stars as you go. Let the final clue lead them to the "baby Jesus". When you find him, sing a song of praise, then celebrate a successful conclusion with a bowl of ice cream! (Put some star sprinkles on top!) Suggested clues – There are various websites which give ideas on clue writing and clue giving specifically for scavenger hunts or if you're feeling creative you can make up your own.

"Digging Deeper": Research

- Jesus' gifts – The wise men gave little Jesus gold, frankincense, and myrrh. We all know what gold is, but what are frankincense and myrrh? What would they be used for? What do they look like? Why were they valuable?

- The wise men – How many were there? We don't know for certain because the Bible doesn't tell us. Research who these men were. Where might they have come from? What skill were they known for? What kind of men were they? How long might their journey have taken to reach Jesus?

"Food For Thought": Puzzles

- Word Scramble – Unscramble the letters to make a word from this lesson. Answers are in the Answer Key.

  b h e l h e t e m _____   h o d r e _____

  t s r a _____   h w r p s i o _____

  o g l d _____   r m y h r _____

  e i r e n n c n k s f a _____   d a m e r _____

  p e t g y _____   n g l e a _____

  r l a i s e _____   g e i e a l l _____

  n a r e z h t a_____   o h j s e p _____

  n i m e e s w _____ _____   g t i s f _____

  r e c b s i s _____   h e o s u _____

- Matching – Match the word or phrase on the left to its answer on the right. Answers are in the Answer Key.

1. City of Jesus' birth	Galilee
2. Where the wise men were from	Judea
3. Jewish king at the time of Jesus' birth	Bethlehem
4. Heavenly guide	Nazareth
5. Gifts for Jesus	Herod
6. Warning	Unknown
7. Country Jesus' family fled to	The East
8. Number of wise men	Archelaus
9. City where Jesus grew up	Ruler
10. Region Bethlehem is located in	Gold, frankincense, myrrh
11. Region Nazareth is located in	Egypt
12. Herod's son	Star
13. Number of gifts Jesus was given	Three
14. Prophesied to come out of Bethlehem	Jerusalem
15. City the wise men arrived in	Dream

 "Fruits Of Our Labor": Crafts

- Gifts for Jesus – Recreate the gifts the wise men brought to Jesus and add your own. You will need a few rocks, gold paint, a couple of incense sticks, a small plastic bottle with a cap, cooking oil, myrrh oil (optional) and a decorated box or basket. Paint the rocks with gold paint and let them dry. Fill the small bottle with cooking oil and add a few drops of the myrrh oil to it for scent. Place the "gold", "frankincense", and "myrrh" in the box or basket. Tie on a label that says, "To Jesus", then think about what gift you'd like to give him and place it in the box or basket. If it's something like "an obedient heart", make a clay heart with the word "obedience" etched in it or draw and color it on paper. Be thoughtful and creative!

- Star of Bethlehem – You will need card stock, glow-in-the-dark paint, some fishing line or string, and the star templates found in Appendix B in the back of the book. Use the star templates to trace onto card stock. Cut them out and punch a hole near the top point to run string or fishing line through later. Paint the stars with glow-in-the-dark paint, then let dry. Assemble the star: Fold each star in half vertically (from top to bottom). Glue all of the stars together with all of the folded edges facing the middle so that you have a 3-dimensional star. Run string through the holes at the top and hang in your bedroom or other room with the lights on for a few hours, then turn off the lights! Just as the star guided the wise men to Jesus, let your star remind you to let the Word of God guide you to Jesus.

Lesson 4: Jesus' Childhood

Text: Luke 2:39-52

"Growing In The Word": Text And Discussion

Read Luke 2:39-40. After leaving Egypt, Joseph, Mary and Jesus return to their home country to settle in the city of Nazareth in the region of Galilee. As Jesus grew, he was filled with God's grace and wisdom and spirit. What kind of child do you think he was? How do you think he acted toward his parents, siblings, and other people?

Read Luke 2:41-42. Do you remember what Passover was? It was when the 10th plague (death of the firstborn) occurred in Egypt while the Israelites were enslaved. The faithful Jews placed the blood of a lamb on their doorposts as the Lord "passed over" their homes, sparing the lives of their firstborn. Immediately after the plague, the pharaoh set the Jews free and let them go as God had commanded him. The Jews held a Passover feast every year to remember this event and the feast lasted 7 days. Passover was one of three Jewish feasts that all faithful Jewish males were required to travel to Jerusalem for each year. Jesus' family, being faithful Jews, went to Jerusalem to celebrate this feast. How old is Jesus at this time? (12)

Read Luke 2:43-45. Jesus' parents did not know he stayed behind in Jerusalem when they left to go home. How could this be? Wouldn't your parents realize you weren't with them if your family went on a trip? In ancient times, many people traveled in large groups or caravans for safety reasons. Apparently this was the case with Mary and Joseph as the Bible says they were looking for Jesus among all their relatives and acquaintances at the end of the first day's journey. They probably assumed he was somewhere in the group walking and talking with friends during the day, but in the evening they couldn't find him anywhere. How do you think they felt? Of course they're very alarmed and head straight back to Jerusalem to look for their child.

Read Luke 2:46-47. How many days did Mary and Joseph spend looking for Jesus? (Three) Where was Jesus this whole time? (In the temple) Why was Jesus there and was he being disobedient to his parents? No, he was taking advantage of the opportunity to hear the great teachers of the law (Mosaic law) while in the capital city of Jerusalem. He was not teaching his elders as he was still a child, but he was listening to them and asking questions. The Jewish teachers, or rabbis, were amazed at how much he understood. Even at a young age, Jesus showed a great interest in the Word of God. It was more important to him than anything else. He serves as a good example to us to value the Bible dearly and to want to hear it taught and talked about more than anything else, even when we're young.

Read Luke 2:48-50. His parents were naturally relieved to find him, but wondered why he'd chosen to stay behind in Jerusalem and cause them so much anxiety. The answer Jesus gave them basically says they shouldn't have been surprised to find him in the temple. It was the natural place for him to be as he was going about his "Father's business." What father

was he talking about? (His Father, God)

Read Luke 2:51-52. They all returned to Nazareth where Jesus lived as an obedient son. Then the Bible says that he grew in wisdom (the ability to make right, godly decisions), and stature (he grew up physically, got taller), and in favor with God and man (both God and people were pleased with him). Are you growing up the same way as Jesus? Are you trying to be wise, pleasing to God, kind to other people, and obedient to your parents?

Review Questions: (Answers are in the Answer Key.)

1. What city did Jesus live in?

2. What was he filled with?

3. What city did his family travel to?

4. What was the occasion?

5. How old was Jesus at this time?

6. Did his parents know he'd stayed behind when they started for home?

7. Where was he?

8. What was he doing there?

9. How long did his parents look for him?

10. What did Jesus say he was doing?

11. Was Jesus an obedient son?

12. What were the three ways Jesus grew?

"Putting Down Roots": Memory Work

- Memorize Luke 2:40

- Memorize Luke 2:52

"Farther Afield": Map Work

Map 1

- Locate the city of Jerusalem – What region is it located in?

"Harvest Fun": Games And Activities

- Locate the Leaven – The evening before the Passover feast began, the head of the family would lead his family through the house by candlelight, searching for leaven. No leaven of any kind was allowed to be in the house during the length of the Passover feast which was 7 days. Sometimes Jewish families would sell their leaven to their Gentile neighbors for the length of Passover, then buy it back when Passover was over. Leaven is any kind of agent, like yeast or baking powder, that causes bread to rise. Hide a package of yeast in the house or write the word "leaven" on a small index card and hide it. Use a battery operated candle or a flashlight to let everyone else search the house to locate the leaven. Take turns hiding it, or hide several and see who can find the most.

- Search for Jesus – Pick one person to be Jesus and have him hide. Everyone searches until they find him. Remember Jesus' parents couldn't find him for three days! He wasn't hiding though, he was spending his time in the temple listening to the Jewish teachers and asking questions.

 ## "Digging Deeper": Research

- Feast of Passover – What event did this commemorate? What foods were eaten? How long did the feast last? What rituals did they practice? Research the Feast of Passover during the time of Christ. It is somewhat different than how Jews celebrate it today.

- Education of Jewish boys in Bible times – What would Jesus' childhood have been like as a Jewish boy? How would he have been educated? What would he have learned and when concerning religion, occupation, etc. At what age would Jewish boys apprentice to their fathers or someone else? What scriptures were they taught and by whom?

"Food For Thought": Puzzles

• Word Search Puzzle - Answers are in the Answer Key.

```
E L P M E T L S D D A E E
M W O B E D I E N T N Q J
E T I R I P S H I M U O O
G N I D N A T S R E D N U
S T E G E E E G S L P P R
G A S R R N N T X A A R N
S R C A N X I O U S R M E
W N Z C E O N J S U E O Y
I A T E N F G O A R N D R
N E R S A T V L T E T S O
T E A C H E R S E J S I V
D V E E R U T A T S E W A
R A H T W E L V E S E S F
```

Nazareth
wisdom
Passover
listening
anxious
heart
stature

Jerusalem
grace
twelve
questions
obedient
increased
teachers

spirit
feast
temple
understanding
favor
journey
parents

- Rebus Puzzle – Can you figure out the message written below? Try to solve it and write your answer at the bottom of the page. Answer is in the Answer Key.

CAN – C + D   T + ♥ – A R T

CH + 👁 + L D   🍇 – A P S + W

CAN – C + D   🐝 – E + 🐫 – L

STOP – O P + R + 1 – E + G

🌧 – R A   S + ⬆ – U + I R + I T.

🔔 – B E L + U + K E   3-1:20+20

"Fruits Of Our Labor": Crafts

• Passover placemat – Cut a piece of poster board 18 inches long by 10 inches wide. Draw and color or paint some of the Passover foods on the placemat. If you have space, write the portion of Exodus 12:27 which says, "It is the sacrifice of the Lord's Passover, for he passed over the houses of the people of Israel in Egypt, when he slew the Egyptians but spared our houses." When you have finished decorating your placemat, laminate it or cover it with clear contact paper to preserve it and make it washable.

• Bake unleavened bread – Unleavened bread was served at the Passover feast. This bread would be very flat since there was no leaven to make the dough rise.

<u>Unleavened bread</u>

1 cup all-purpose flour $\frac{1}{2}$ tsp. salt, or as needed (optional)

1/3 cup water, or more if needed   1 tsp. olive oil, or as needed

Move an oven rack near the top of the oven and preheat oven to 475 degrees. Preheat a heavy baking sheet in the oven. Set the timer for 16 minutes (18 max). Dust a clean work surface and a rolling pin with flour. Place the flour into a mixing bowl. Pour the water into the flour one tablespoon at a time and stir with a fork until the dough forms a rough ball. Remove the dough to the prepared work surface, knead rapidly and firmly until smooth, about 30 seconds to 1 minute. Divide the dough into four equal pieces; cut each piece in half again to get 8 pieces total. Swiftly roll each piece into a ball. Roll each piece of dough out into a 5-inch pancake, dusting the top and rolling pin with flour as needed. Gradually roll the pancakes out to a size of about 8 inches, increasing the size of each by about 1 inch, then letting the dough rest for a few seconds before rolling again to the finished size. Roll from the center out. The bread rounds should be very thin. Using a fork, quickly pierce each bread all over, about 25 times, to prevent rising. The holes should go completely through the bread. Flip the bread over, and pierce each piece another 25 times with the fork. With at least 5 minutes left on the timer, remove the hot baking sheet from the preheated oven and place the dough rounds onto the baking sheet. Place the baking sheet onto the rack near the top of the oven and bake for 2 minutes; turn the rounds over and bake for 2 minutes more, until the bread rounds are lightly browned and crisp. Transfer to a wire rack to cool. Lightly brush olive oil onto each round and, if desired, sprinkle with salt.

Lesson 5: Baptism of Jesus

Text: Matthew 3:1-17

"Growing In The Word": Lesson Text And Discussion

Read Matthew 3:1-3. Where was John preaching? (Wilderness of Judea) What was he preaching? (Repentance) This was the mission he was called to. The prophet Isaiah had prophesied that there would be a forerunner or someone who would prepare the way for Jesus' ministry. (Isaiah 40:3)

Read Matthew 3:4. What was John dressed like and what did he eat? (He wore camel's hair with a leather belt and he ate locusts and wild honey.) The prophet Elijah in the Old Testament is described as wearing similar clothing as John. Would you like to wear camel's hair? It might be a little scratchy! He lived a simple life in the wilderness. He's not distracted with worldly things like expensive clothes or fancy feasts, but rather he has one focus: preaching to prepare the way for Jesus.

Read Matthew 3:5-6. Many people were coming to hear this simple preacher and to be baptized by him. He was baptizing in the Jordan River (by immersion) and people were repenting and confessing their sins. What does repentance mean? Many think it means being sorry for sin, but it's more than that. Being sorry is a start, but then you need to make changes in your life; stop sinning and turn to God. That's true repentance. What does "confess" mean? To confess your sins means to "say the same thing". For example, God says that it is a sin to lie. If you tell a lie and confess, you are saying you sinned because you told a lie. It's kind of like when a criminal is arrested and he makes a confession. He admits to the police, "Yes, I robbed that bank". God wants us to see sin for what it is and be willing to admit when we've done wrong so that we can repent (change) and do what's right.

Read Matthew 3:7-12. Some Pharisees and Sadducees came to hear John and he had some fiery preaching to direct at them! First of all, who were the Pharisees and Sadducees? These two groups were the ruling religious class in Israel. The Sadducees tended to be wealthy and powerful and tried hard to keep peace with Rome. They didn't relate very well to the common man. The Pharisees related more to the common people and were looked up to by them. However, they tended to be arrogant and self-righteous (we're better than you!). What does John call them? (Brood of vipers – a viper is a poisonous snake) He then says they should "bear fruits worthy of repentance." What do you think he meant by that? John is telling them that fake religion doesn't cut it. You have to show your repentance and dedication to God in the way you live your life. The Pharisees and Sadducees thought that since they were Jews and had Abraham as their ancestor, they were "safe" with God and could act any way they wanted. Not so! John's words about unfruitful trees being cut down and the chaff of wheat being burned up are symbolic of what happens to those who refuse to truly repent and obey God.

Read Matthew 3:13-15. Remember, Jesus lived in Nazareth in Galilee. He traveled to Judea to meet up with John, but John doesn't want to baptize Jesus. Why is that? (John doesn't feel he's worthy, or good enough, to baptize Jesus.) Jesus urges him to. Jesus is the sinless son of God so why does he need to be baptized? He does it to "fulfill all righteousness." That means he's going to do everything that is right, so he considered being baptized as something that's right to do. Then John baptized Jesus in the Jordan River.

Read Matthew 3:16-17. As Jesus came up out of the water, God's Spirit descended in what form? (A dove) And the voice of God said, "This is my beloved Son in whom I'm well pleased." It was important for everyone there to see and hear this. Jesus is now about 30 years old, getting ready to start his ministry and at the beginning of it, God is declaring, "This is my Son!"

Review Questions: (Answers are in the Answer Key.)

1. Where was John the Baptist preaching?

2. What was he preaching?

3. What prophet spoke about him being a "voice crying in the wilderness"?

4. Describe John's clothing.

5. What did John eat?

6. Where did he baptize people?

7. What two groups of people came to hear him and got a fiery sermon?

8. What part of Jesus' clothing did John say he wasn't even worth to carry?

9. Where did Jesus travel from to come to John?

10. Why did Jesus want to be baptized?

11. In what form did the Spirit of God descend upon Jesus?

12. What did God say?

 ## "Putting Down Roots": Memory Work

- Memorize Matthew 3:17

- Memorize Isaiah 40:3

"Farther Afield": Map Work

Map 1

- Locate the Jordan River – How many miles long is it?

 ## "Harvest Fun": Games And Activities

- Jesus or John – Each player needs to have two index cards for this game. On one card write the name "Jesus". On the other card, write the name "John". As the following questions are asked by one selected person, each player must hold up the card with the correct answer. Be careful! There may be some trick questions! You may keep score if you'd like.

1. I am a Nazarene. (Jesus)

2. My mother's name is Elizabeth. (John)

3. I am a preacher. (Both!)

4. I was baptizing people in the Jordan River. (John)

5. My mother's name is Mary. (Jesus)

6. I was baptized to fulfill all righteousness. (Jesus)

7. I eat bugs! (John)

8. My father spoke at my baptism. (Jesus)

9. I wear clothes made out of camel's hair. (John)

10. I am a Jew. (Both!)

11. I live in the wilderness of Judea. (John)

12. I live in Galilee. (Jesus)

13. I was sent to prepare the way of the Lord. (John)

14. I was prophesied about in the Old Testament. (Both!)

15. A dove alighted on me. (Jesus)

- Act it Out – Act out the scene of the baptism. You will need at least two people; one to be Jesus and one to be John. You may want to make a recording of God's voice saying, "This is my beloved Son in whom I am well pleased," to be played at the proper time. Think of what props you will need or any scenery you may like to have. Video your production if you'd like!

 ## "Digging Deeper": Research

- John the Baptist – Find out more about John the Baptist. Who were his parents and what were the circumstances of his birth? Who was he related to? What was he like? Was he a Nazarite? What was a Nazarite?

- Pharisees and Sadducees – Learn more about these two religious groups of Jesus' day. How did they get started and what did they each believe? In what ways were they similar? In what ways were they different?

- Baptism: A study – Was Jesus immersed, sprinkled, or had water poured on his head? What was the baptism of John for? Why was Jesus baptized? How are we baptized today and what is baptism for? Look up these scriptures and write what you learn about the subject of baptism: Acts 2:38; Acts 8:36-38; Acts 22:16; Romans 6:3,4; Titus 3:5; I Peter 3:21.

 ## "Food For Thought": Puzzles

- Coded Message -

| 7 | 19 | 18 | 8 | | 18 | 8 | | 14 | 2 | | 25 | 22 | 15 | 12 | 5 | 22 | 23 |

| 8 | 12 | 13 | | 18 | 13 | | 4 | 19 | 12 | 14 | | 18 | | 26 | 14 |

| 4 | 22 | 15 | 15 | | 11 | 15 | 22 | 26 | 8 | 22 | 23 |

Key to the Code:

F	N	R	U	A	G	O	S	V	C	H	T	D	I	E	B	W	K	Y	P	M	L	J
21	13	9	6	26	20	12	8	5	24	19	7	23	18	22	25	4	16	2	11	14	15	17

- Crossword Puzzle – Answers are in the Answer Key.

Across

1 Where John was preaching
5 Region where he preached
7 A voice spoke from here
11 Animal hair of John's clothing
12 John the Baptist preached this
13 God said, "This is my beloved ____"
15 Name of river John baptized in
16 Old Testament book with prophecy about John

Down

2 Kind of belt John wore
3 Jesus was baptized to fulfill all
4 The ____ of God descended like a dove
6 Where Jesus traveled from to be baptized
8 What the Spirit of God descended like
9 Kind of bug that John ate
10 John said he wasn't worthy to carry Jesus' ____
14 He baptized Jesus

"Fruits Of Our Labor": Crafts

- Model dove – Using white play-doh or clay, sculpt a dove. You could use white craft feathers to push into the clay for wings if you'd like. In our lesson, the Spirit of God descended on Jesus like a dove after he was baptized.

- John the Baptist picture -Draw or paint a picture of John the Baptist. Remember how he dressed, where he lived, and what he ate!

Lesson 6: Temptation of Jesus

Text: Matthew 4:1-11; Luke 4:1-13

"Growing In The Word": Lesson Text And Discussion

*Only the Matthew text will be listed here for discussion, but you are encouraged to read both texts for this lesson to give a fuller picture of this event.

Read Matthew 4:1. Notice who led Jesus into the wilderness – the Spirit of God, but who is going to tempt him? (The devil) Anytime we face temptations, they are from the devil. James 1:13 tells us that God *never* tempts us to do evil. It's also interesting to note that Jesus is tempted just shortly after his baptism. Sometimes we're hit with temptations when we think we're spiritually strong and Satan wants to weaken us. Be on guard!

Read Matthew 4:2-3. Jesus knew what was coming so he fasted for forty days and forty nights to prepare himself. What does it mean to fast? (It is going without food or eating only a very little food for a specified amount of time.) There are different reasons for fasting, but one of the purposes is to focus solely on God and spiritual things. Jesus was probably spending a lot of these forty days in prayer to his heavenly Father. The Bible says he was hungry after fasting. Can you imagine not eating for forty days? You'd be very hungry too! What was the very first temptation? (Turning stones to bread) Satan knows exactly what to try to tempt us with. He knows where we are likely to be weak and tries to use it against us. Jesus is going to answer every temptation the same way – with the word of God.

Read Matthew 4:4. Jesus answers Satan's temptation with a passage from Deuteronomy 8:3. Remember that in the time of Jesus, the only "Bible" they had was the Old Testament. The books of the New Testament were not written until after Jesus' death. The first word Satan uses is "if." He is throwing doubt on the fact that Jesus is the Son of God – even though the voice of God had just declared him to be so after he was baptized. Satan is basically saying, "So, you're the Son of God? Prove it!"

Read Matthew 4:5-6. Satan now tempts Jesus to throw himself down from atop of the temple to again prove that he is the Son of God. Satan cleverly uses scripture himself to remind Jesus that God won't let anything happen to him, soooo, "If you're the Son of God...", but Jesus answers him in verse 7.

Read Matthew 4:7. What scripture did Jesus use to answer Satan? ("You shall not tempt the Lord your God.")

Read Matthew 4:8,9. The devil now tempts Jesus by showing him all the kingdoms of the world and their glory and says to him, "This can all be yours! If...you worship me." Satan and God both desire to be worshiped by man but for very different reasons. God is holy and good and we worship Him because as the Creator and Lord, He is worthy of worship. Satan seeks to be worshiped for his own vain glory. He is selfish and prideful.

Read Matthew 4:10. Jesus rebukes or scolds Satan again by using scripture. Jesus knows that only the Lord God is to be worshiped and served. Jesus commands Satan to get away from him. After Satan left Jesus, who came to minister to him? (Angels)

Read Matthew 4:11. Jesus stayed strong in the Lord and in His Word and did not give in to any of Satan's temptations. Every time he was tempted, he used the word of God to combat it. That is why it is so important to memorize scripture: so it will always be in our heart and ready to call to our minds when we're faced with temptations. David said in Psalm 119:11, *"Thy word have I hid in my heart that I might not sin against Thee."* Let us all try hard to follow Jesus' example.

*Further Food for Thought: I John 2:16 talks about the three kinds of temptations that Satan uses - lust of the flesh, lust of the eye, and the pride of life. He used all three of them on Jesus:

1. *Lust of the flesh – Turning stones to bread to satisfy his hunger

2. Lust of the eye - "All these kingdoms can be yours!"

3. Pride of life – Jesus could throw himself off the top of the temple and not even get hurt because being God's Son, he's special.

Satan still uses these same tactics against us, so let's stay strong in the Lord and in the power of His word!

*Lust – a wrong desire

Review Questions: (Answers are in the Answer Key.)

1. Who led Jesus to the wilderness?

2. How long did Jesus fast?

3. Who came to tempt Jesus?

4. What was the first temptation?

5. How did Jesus respond?

6. What was the second temptation?

7. How did Jesus respond?

8. What was the third temptation?

9. How did Jesus respond?

10. Who came to minister to Jesus after the devil left him?

11. What does John say are the three types of temptation?

"Putting Down Roots": Memory Work

- Memorize Psalm 119:11
- Memorize Matthew 4:4, 4:7, and 4:10

 ### "Farther Afield": Map Work

Map 1

- Draw a small symbol of the temple and place it near the city of Jerusalem.

 ### "Harvest Fun": Games And Activities

- Resist the Temptation! - Think of some different scenarios where you'd be faced with a temptation or choice to make and write them down. Take turns reading these aloud and allow others to answer how they'd resist the temptation. Remember to use scripture when you can as Jesus did. For example, if the scenario suggests you could tell a lie to cover something up, you might respond that God's word says, "You shall not lie". A good card game for this is called "Choices - Kid's Pocket Card Game" for ages 6-11. It costs around $6.00 and is available online and at Christian bookstores. There is also a teen version for ages 13-19.

- Scripture Race – Use one of the three scripture responses Jesus used against Satan and write it out one word per index card. For two players or two teams, you will need two different colors of index cards, one color per player or team. Let one person (not playing the game) hide the word cards all over the room (or house). For example, taped to the bottom of a chair, in a window, under a cushion, etc. When "Go!" is called, the players race to find all of the word cards in their color and then correctly assemble the scripture on the floor or table. The first player or team to collect all of their cards and correctly assemble the verse wins!

"Digging Deeper": Research

- Biblical Fasting – Jesus fasted for forty days and nights in the wilderness before Satan came to tempt him. Learn about the different ways in which people fasted and for what reasons. What were they allowed or not allowed to eat/drink? How long did the fasts last?

- Temple Architecture – Satan took Jesus to the "pinnacle of the temple" in Jerusalem. This was not Solomon's temple, as it had been destroyed by King Nebuchadnezzar and the Babylonians around 586 B.C. The temple, in Jesus' day, had been rebuilt by King Herod. What did it look like? How did it compare or contrast with the temple of Solomon? Where was the pinnacle?

- Who was Satan? - Research the origins of Satan and what happened to him. How do you think he knew the scriptures? Did simply knowing the scriptures mean he valued them and used them correctly?

"Food For Thought": Puzzles

- Word Scramble – Unscramble the following words from this lesson. Answers are in the Answer Key.

s u e j e	_____	n d l s i e w r s e	_____
d p t m e t e	_____	e f a t s d	_____
v i l e d	_____	n o s t e s	_____
r e a d b	_____	n i p a l e c n	_____
m e p t l e	_____	g s l a n e	_____
m s k g n o i d	_____	p r o s h i w	_____

- Scripture Matching – Match the following scriptures to their correct reference. Answers are in the Answer Key.

1. Man shall not live by bread alone...

2. Blessed are the pure in heart...

3. For God so loved the world...

4. In the beginning, God created...

5. He makes me to lie down in green pastures...

6. This is My beloved Son...

7. And Jesus increased in wisdom and stature...

8. For with God, nothing will be impossible...

9. For there is born to you this day...

10. You shall love the Lord your God...

Matthew 3:17

Luke 2:11

Deuteronomy 6:5

John 3:16

Luke 2:52

Deuteronomy 8:3

Matthew 5:8

Genesis 1:1

Luke 1:37

Psalm 23:2

 "Fruits Of Our Labor": Crafts

- Storyboard – Take a piece of poster board or large piece of paper and divide it into three sections. Draw the three temptations of Jesus, scene by scene. When you're finished, show it to someone and tell them the story of the temptation of Jesus.

- Mobile – Make a mobile with symbols to remind you of this lesson. You will need a wire coat hanger, some string or yarn, glue or tape, drawing paper and drawing materials. First, draw three symbols of the temptations: 1) a stone or loaf of bread, 2) the temple, 3) a tall mountain. After they're drawn, color them then cut them out. Punch a small hole at the top of each picture. Cut three lengths of string or yarn. You might want them different lengths so your pictures don't overlap. Tie a piece of string or yarn through the hole in each picture, then tie the other end to the bottom wire of the hanger. Last, draw and color a picture of an open Bible, nice and large. Cut it out, then tape it at the top of the hanger (below the hook). Hang the mobile in your room or other prominent place where it can remind you of what temptations Jesus faced and how he overcame them. With the help of the Lord and the power of His word, you can overcome temptation too!

Lesson 7: Jesus Calls Disciples

Text: Luke 5:1-11, 27-28; John 1:35-49

"Growing In God's Word": Lesson Text And Discussion

What is a disciple? A disciple is simply a student or follower. Jesus is about to begin his earthly ministry and he now starts to call disciples to follow him. Some of these men will become the 12 apostles.

Read Luke 5:1-3. Where did Jesus teach the people from? (A boat) Why do you think he did this? There were so many people pressing about him to try to hear him speak that he had to get in a boat and put out to sea a little ways in order to be better seen and heard by the crowd. Whose boat did he use? (Simon's)

Read Luke 5:4-7. How long had Simon and the other fishermen been fishing? (All night long) When Jesus told them to let down their nets again, Simon didn't see the point in trying anymore. He'd been fishing for hours without catching a single thing, but he did it anyway because Jesus told him to. Sometimes we get discouraged or tired of doing something that doesn't seem to be working, but if it's something God is commanding us to do, then we need to be obedient and trust in Him and His help. When Simon obeyed Jesus, what happened? (His fishing nets were so full, he needed help pulling them in!)

Read Luke 5:8-11. Jesus told Simon Peter and his partners, James and John, that from now on they were going to be fishers of men. What did he mean? They're now going to follow Jesus and help teach men about the Lord. Their "catch" will be the hearts and souls of men.

Read Luke 5:27-28. Levi is another name for Matthew, the same writer of the book of Matthew in the New Testament. As a tax collector, he worked for the Roman government. His job did <u>not</u> make him popular with the Jewish people. What did he leave to follow Jesus? (Everything) What are we willing to give up to follow Jesus? Is it easy or hard to sacrifice something for Jesus?

Read John 1:35-42. John the Baptist had been preaching in the wilderness and had disciples of his own who were waiting for the Messiah. When John saw Jesus and said, "Behold the Lamb of God!", two of John's disciples followed Jesus. One of them, Andrew, went to tell his brother Simon. This is the same Simon Peter whose boat Jesus would preach from. Andrew was so excited to find the Messiah and he wanted to share the good news! We should also want to share the good news of Jesus with others.

Read John 1:43-49. Jesus wanted to return to the region of Galilee where he was from. He found Philip and told him to follow him. Who else was from the same city as Philip? (Andrew and Peter) Philip also shared the good news with his friend, Nathanael. When Jesus saw Nathanael, he said a couple of interesting things. First, he said Nathanael was an honest man (no guile or deceit was in him). Second, Jesus told him he knew him already and had seen him sitting under a fig tree before Philip called him. Nathanael is amazed at this and immediately calls Jesus two things. What are they? (Son of God, King of Israel)

Do you, like Nathanael, believe that Jesus is the Son of God? I pray you do!

<u>Review Questions</u>: (Answers are in the Answer Key.)

1. What lake was Jesus standing by in Luke 5?

2. Whose boat did he get into?

3. How long had Simon Peter and his partners been fishing?

4. How much had they caught?

5. What happened when Jesus told them to cast their nets out again?

6. What brothers were fishing partners of Simon Peter?

7. Jesus said he would make the fishermen fishers of what?

8. What did Peter, James and John leave to follow Jesus?

9. What is Levi's other name?

10. What was Levi's occupation?

11. What did Levi leave behind to follow Jesus?

12. Who was a disciple of John the Baptist who then followed Jesus?

13. What city was Philip from?

14. Whom did Philip go and tell about Jesus?

15. Where did Jesus see Nathanael before Philip called him?

16. What two things does Nathanael call Jesus?

 ## "Putting Down Roots": Memory Work

- Memorize Luke 5:28

- Memorize John 1:49

- Memorize the 12 apostles: Peter, Andrew, James, John, Philip, Thomas, Matthew, Bartholomew, James the less, Simon, Thaddeus, Judas

"Farther Afield": Map Work

Map 1

- Locate the city of Bethsaida
- Locate the Lake of Gennesaret

 ## "Harvest Fun": Games And Activities

- Go Fish! - (One of the craft activities will need to be completed in order to play this game.) Use your fish and fishing rod previously made. Let an adult write a review question or memory verse reference on each fish. Place the fish in a "pond". This could be several sheets of blue paper placed on the floor, a blue bed sheet, kiddie pool, or something more elaborate that you create! Take your fishing pole and "catch" a fish. See if you can answer the question or recite the verse. If you get it right, that fish is a keeper. If you answer incorrectly, you must throw it back in the pond. You can play this with individual players or in two teams, keeping score as to the most correct answers.

- Tell a friend about Jesus – In John 1:35-49, we see that Andrew went and told his brother Simon about Jesus, and Philip told his friend, Nathanael. Find a friend or family member who needs to know Jesus. Share with them what you've learned and invite them to study the Bible with you or your family to learn more about Jesus together.

 ## "Digging Deeper": Research

- The Twelve Apostles – Some of the apostles were first called by Jesus in this lesson. If you memorized the names of all twelve, do some research about them to see what you can learn. Notice they were from different places, had different occupations, and different personalities and abilities. Jesus sees each of us as unique and with specific talents and abilities to serve Him.

- Tax Collectors – Levi, or Matthew, was called by Jesus and he was a tax collector. See what you can learn about tax collectors in the time of Jesus. Who employed them? What exactly did they do? Why did the population at large dislike them so much? Who was another famous tax collector in the New Testament?

"Food For Thought": Puzzles

- Guess the Disciple – Read the following clues and see if you can guess which disciple it is. Each name is used twice. Answers are in the Answer Key.

1. I am a tax collector. _____

2. My brother's name is Simon. _____

3. I told my friend to come and see Jesus. _____

4. I was sitting under a fig tree. _____

5. James is my brother. _____

6. Besides John, I'm another son of Zebedee. _____

7. I'm a fisherman and Andrew is my brother. _____

8. My other name is Levi. _____

9. Like Peter and Andrew, I'm from the city of Bethsaida. _____

10. Jesus said He'd call me Cephas. _____

11. I called Jesus the Son of God and King of Israel. _____

12. I was a disciple of John the Baptist. _____

13. We are brothers and fishing partners of Simon Peter. _____

- Word Search Puzzle – On the following page is a word search puzzle. Answers are in the Answer Key.

```
S C F F O L L O W T A N S W L L S
A D I A S H T E B R O T H E R S U
H I S G M A H Z A I H L S O M E S
P S H H O T E B A N D R E W J A E
E C E B T B B S I A A C E V Z B J
C I R A E I I P I L I H P F I J H
T P M D E M T E M E E R T G I F H
A L E R O T C E L L O C X A T L E
G E N N E S A R E T O S E E N H S
```

fishermen
follow
Bethsaida
Zebedee
Levi
Jesus

Simon
Andrew
boat
Rabbi
Matthew

James
disciple
Gennesaret
Cephas
tax collector

John
Philip
Nathanael
fig tree
brothers

"Fruits Of Our Labor": Crafts

- Go Fish! - You will be making items needed for the "Go Fish!" game. Use different colors of construction paper to draw and cut out several fish shapes. Make them different sizes and shapes, or you may use the fish templates in Appendix B if you would like. Take a dowel rod and cut it into an 18-inch length. Secure the end of a piece of string to one end of the dowel rod with glue or strong tape. Wind the string around the end of the rod several times and secure with glue. Leave a 24-inch length of string hanging down. Glue a small magnet to the end of the hanging string. Place paper clips on the end of each paper fish. Now your fish are ready to be caught!

- Make a moneybag with gold coins – Matthew was a tax collector. He went around collecting the tax money that the people had to pay to the Roman government. Most of the money would have been in coins. To make the coins: Use a real quarter, nickel, dime, and penny to trace several "coins" onto card stock or poster board. Paint the back and front of the "coins" with gold paint, let it dry, (or you may color them with a gold crayon) then cut them out. To make the money bag: Copy the money bag template from Appendix B onto heavy card stock. Color or paint it if desired. Fold the two halves together. Punch holes where indicated. Take a 24-inch piece of yarn and tightly wrap one end with tape to make it easy to thread the holes. Whip stitch the money bag on each side, then knot each end of the yarn, or tuck the ends inside and secure them with tape. Trim excess yarn. Fill your bag with the coins.

Lesson 8: Jesus' First Miracle

Text: John 2:1-12

"Growing In God's Word": Lesson Text And Discussion

Read John 2:1-2. This event takes place three days after Jesus called his first disciples. His family and disciples were invited to attend a wedding celebration in the city of Cana. What region is Cana in? (Galilee)

Read John 2:3-5. Can you imagine attending a wedding where they run out of cake before everybody gets a piece? Well, running out of wine at a wedding in Bible times would be just as embarrassing! Jesus' mother, Mary, tells her son because she knows he can do something about it. Jesus' answer is not being disrespectful to his mother, but rather is giving a gentle rebuke. She wanted him to make himself known as the Messiah, but "His hour was not yet come". In other words, this wasn't the proper time for that yet. Mary isn't offended, she simply instructs the servants to do whatever her son says.

Read John 2:6-8. The waterpots that Jesus commanded to be filled with water were huge. How much water could each one hold? (20-30 gallons) Look at a gallon of milk or orange juice in your refrigerator and imagine 20 or 30 of them in one big stone jar! How many of these water pots were there? (6) Jesus commanded the servants to fill them all with water and then to draw some out and take it to someone. Who was it? (The master of the feast) It was a Jewish custom at weddings to designate one guest as a "ruler" or "master" of the wedding celebration.

Read John 2:9-10. The master doesn't know what has taken place, but someone else does. Who knows what Jesus has done? (The servants) The master thinks the bridegroom has been holding out on the guests and saved the best wine for last.

Read John 2:11-12. This first miracle that Jesus' disciples see creates belief in them. Miracles had a very specific purpose in the Bible – they were to confirm the Word of God. When a prophet, apostle, or Jesus Himself gave a message from the Lord, or a sermon or some teaching and then later performed a miracle, it served as a confirmation that what the person said was true. Where did Jesus, his family, and his disciples move onto from here? (Capernaum)

*A note about Biblical wine. Many people believe that drinking wine is acceptable since Jesus made wine himself. However, the wine we have today differs greatly from wine in Biblical times. Not all wines in the Bible were alcoholic and those that were had different alcoholic content than our wines today. In fact, what the Bible refers to as "strong drink" would be an equivalent of our modern day wine. The Greek word for wine in this passage is *oinos* which can mean fermented or unfermented grape juice. In New Testament times, the best wines were considered to be those whose alcoholic content had been removed by boiling or filtration. According to ancient authors like Pliny, Plutarch and Horace, the best wines were harmless and innocent, "destitute of spirit" (had no intoxicating alcohol). So the wine that

Jesus made was exceptional because it was new and freshly made. Another point to consider - why would Jesus, being the Son of God, create 120 – 180 gallons of intoxicating wine so everyone at the wedding feast could get drunk? It would negate the sinlessness of Jesus and his teachings. John 2:11 says this beginning of signs manifested (or made known) His glory. This could not be the case if he had just caused people to stumble and sin by creating intoxicating wine for them.

<u>Review Questions</u>: (Answers are in the Answer Key.)

1. What city were Jesus and his disciples at?

2. What event were they invited to?

3. What did they run out of at the feast?

4. Who turned to Jesus for help?

5. How many waterpots were there?

6. About how many gallons did each waterpot hold?

7. What were the pots made of?

8. Whom did Jesus command the servants to give some wine to?

9. Whom did the master of the feast think had saved the best wine for last?

10. What did this first miracle of Jesus do?

11. What city did Jesus travel to next?

 "Putting Down Roots": Memory Work

- Memorize John 2:11

 "Farther Afield": Map Work

Map 1
- Locate the city of Cana
- Locate the city of Capernaum

"Harvest Fun": Games And Activities"

- Musical Chairs – Music is always a part of weddings. Put on some wedding music or music of your choice and play a lively game of musical chairs!

- Fill those Waterpots! - Place two 5-gallon buckets a few feet apart at one end of the yard. Have two players or two teams race against each other to "fill their waterpot" first. At the starting line (about 20 feet back from the buckets), have two more buckets filled with water along with a ladle for each player or team. On "Go!", let a player fill his ladle with water, race to pour the water in his bucket, then race back to refill or pass it to the next player on his team. Set a time to race and when time's up, the winner is the player or team with the fullest bucket.

"Digging Deeper": Research

- Jewish Wedding Feasts – How were Jewish weddings celebrated in Bible times? What would the wedding feast be like and how long would it last?

- Biblical Wine – How was wine made in Bible times? How was it stored? What would they do to remove alcoholic content? What is fermentation?

"Food For Thought": Puzzles

- Who Am I/What Am I? - Guess the word from the clues given. Answers are in the Answer Key.

1. I am a big event. _____

2. I am made out of stone and can hold 20-30 gallons of liquid. _____

3. The bride couldn't do without me. _____

4. I'm an opportunity for people to eat a lot. _____

5. I'm a drink that was made from water, not grapes. _____

6. I'll wait on you hand and foot. _____

7. My mother wanted me to solve a problem. _____

8. My purpose is to confirm the word of God. _____

9. We went to Cana with Jesus, but we're not members of his family. _____

10. I was a guest at the wedding and knew who to go to when a problem arose. _____

- Crossword Puzzle – Answers are in the Answer Key.

Across

2 She told Jesus about the problem
4 City where Jesus attended an event
5 What kind of event was Jesus at?
9 Next city Jesus visited
10 The ____ wine was saved for last
12 Number of waterpots
13 Jesus' miracles manifested his ____
14 What the waterpots were made of

Down

1 The master of the feast was impressed and called the _____
3 Jesus turned _____ into wine
6 Jesus instructed them to draw the water out
7 The wine was given to the _____ of the feast
8 Each pot could hold 20 to 30 _____
11 What did they run out of at the feast?

"Fruits Of Our Labor": Crafts

- Water to "Wine" - Take a clear glass pitcher and fill it with water. Pour in packets of grape Kool-Aid and stir to watch the water change color. Serve your grape drink with a snack and discuss how Jesus didn't do a magic trick or something that he needed powders or food coloring to do - what he did was a miracle!

- Clay pots - At the wedding feast, Jesus commanded six large stone jars to be filled with water before he changed it to wine. Take modeling clay or play-doh and form six clay pots or jars. Use a plastic knife, toothpick, or carving tool to carve designs on the outside of your pots. You may use these pots as props to help you tell this story of Jesus' first miracle to someone.

Lesson 9: Jesus and the Woman at the Well

Text: John 4:5-42

"Growing In The Word": Lesson Text And Discussion

Read John 4:5-6. It is interesting that Jesus goes into the region of Samaria. If you look at a map of Palestine in the time of Jesus, you will see the region of Judea in the south where the city of Jerusalem is located. Samaria is the region above Judea, and Galilee is the northern region above Samaria. Jesus' was born in Bethlehem of Judea, but grew up in Nazareth of Galilee. Jesus had been spending some time in the region of Judea and now heads to Galilee. The most direct route is through the region of Samaria; however, most Jews would not go this way. The Jews hated the Samaritan people so much that they would take a longer way around to avoid traveling through Samaria, but Jesus doesn't do this. Jesus and his disciples had been traveling for several hours and are now tired and thirsty. What hour of the day is it? (The sixth) Do you know what time that is? The Jews' day went from sunrise to sunset instead of from midnight to midnight like our day. The first hour of the day would begin at dawn or around 6:00 a.m. and the twelfth hour of the day would be sunset or around 6:00 p.m. So, to find out when the sixth hour was, count six hours ahead from 6:00 a.m. Did you figure it out? The time would be 12:00 noon.

Read John 4:7-9. After traveling, Jesus was tired and thirsty just like we get sometimes. He sits down by a well called Jacob's well. A Samaritan woman comes to the well to draw water. What does Jesus ask her for? (A drink of water) The woman is surprised he is talking to her for two reasons: 1) Jews didn't talk to Samaritans unless they absolutely had to, and 2) She's a woman. Jewish men were not usually seen talking with women in public.

Read John 4:10-15. Jesus tells the woman that if she realized who he was, she'd be asking him for living water. What do you think Jesus means by "living water" and can we have it today? Read John 7:37-39 to see what the living water is.

Read John 4:16-19. The woman now goes from calling Jesus "sir" to calling him a prophet because he seems to know all about her and her life – and he does! How many husbands did Jesus say she had had? (5)

Read John 4:20-24. She then starts to talk to Jesus about the proper place to worship since she's a Samaritan and the Samaritans worshiped on Mr. Gerizim and he's a Jew and Jews worshiped at the temple in Jerusalem. He points out to her not to focus on the place of worship but the *way* to worship. How does God desire to be worshiped? (In spirit and in truth) Worship is not to be based on the way we like best or what seems right to us, but rather the way God has set forth in the scriptures.

Read John 4:25-26. The woman then acknowledges that the Messiah is coming and Jesus admits to her that it is He! Can you imagine what she must have thought when she heard this? "I'm standing here talking to the Messiah! The Son of God!"

Read John 4:27. Jesus' disciples come back from town with the food they went to buy and are very surprised to see Jesus talking with this woman – a Samaritan woman! But they don't say anything about it out loud.

Read John 4:28-30. The woman is so excited by her discovery, she can't wait to go share the good news! Do you get excited to share the good news of Jesus Christ with other people? What did she leave and where did she go? (She left her waterpot and went into the city.) After she tells people about her encounter with Jesus, what did the people do? (Went out of the city and came to him)

Read John 4:31-38. Meanwhile, a food discussion. The disciples are focused on actual food while Jesus is talking about spiritual food. He talks to them about the harvest – not of crops, but of souls. Many people needed to hear about Jesus. There was harvesting work to do then and there still is for us today.

Read John 4:39-42. Because of the woman sharing the good news about Jesus, many Samaritans came to him and believed. The Samaritans were so eager to hear the teaching of Jesus that they asked him to stay for awhile. How long did he stay there? (2 days) What did the Samaritans believe after hearing Jesus? "This is indeed the Christ, the Savior of the world." Amen!

Review Questions: (Answers are in the Answer Key.)

1. What region did Jesus and his disciples travel to?

2. What city did they stop at?

3. What did Jesus sit down by?

4. What did the disciples go off to do?

5. What kind of water did Jesus talk about to the woman?

6. How many husbands had the woman had?

7. Was she currently married?

8. What did the woman think Jesus was at first?

9. How did Jesus say people are to worship God?

10. What did Jesus admit to the woman?

11. What did the woman do when she found out who Jesus was?

12. What "harvest" was Jesus talking about?

13. Did very many of the Samaritans believe?

14. What did they all believe?

"Putting Down Roots": Memory Work

- Memorize John 4:13, 14
- Memorize John 4:24

 ## "Farther Afield": Map Work

Map 1

- Locate the region of Samaria
- Locate the city of Sychar
- Locate Mt. Gerizim (mark it with an inverted "V" for a mountain symbol)

 ## "Harvest Fun": Games and Activities

- Race to build a well – This is a game for 2 players or 2 teams. You will need jumbo marshmallows to build the wells and either peanut butter or frosting for the "glue". A less messy alternative is to use toothpicks and small marshmallows. After "Go!" is announced, see who can build a well the fastest in two minutes.

- Find the Living Water – For this game you will need the Water droplets template in Appendix B. Copy the template onto blue paper and cut out the water droplets. (Copy more than one page, if needed.) On one water droplet, write "Living Water". Leave the rest blank. Hide the water droplets then let players race to find the "Living Water". Another variation would be to place all of the water droplets face down on a table, spread out. Have players answer review questions from the lesson. If a player answers correctly, he may pick a water droplet to see if he's found the living water. After playing the game, discuss what the Living Water is that Jesus offered the Samaritan woman and still offers to us today. (John 7:37-39)

"Digging Deeper": Research

- Samaritans – Who were they? Where did they come from? Why did the Jews dislike them so much?

- Jacob's Well – This is the well where Jesus spoke to the Samaritan woman. Where is it located? Who is buried close by? Can you still see this well today?

 ## "Food For Thought": Puzzles

- Word Search Puzzle – Answers are in the Answer Key.

```
R V P V T B C H P D S L I V I N G S
E O N S S S E A U P I H S R O W U N
E U N W Y E E L A S E L P I C S I D
K I O C R R W V I A B W T S E A B L
N W H A R T O P R E T A W J T V B N
I A V L S L M U A A V D N N R I A E
R T L A A L A T M L H E U D S O R V
D E A F O U N T A I N O D H S R O L
W R I E H A I S S E M N O I B S C S
```

Samaria	Sychar	well	water	woman
disciples	Jesus	living	drink	fountain
husbands	mountain	worship	salvation	Messiah
waterpot	Rabbi	harvest	reap	believed
Savior				

- Coded Message -

___ ___ ___ ___   ___ ___   ___ ___ ___ ___   ___ ___ ___ ___
15 18 21 7   6   11   2   12 6   9   22 2   22 8

___ ___ ___   ___ ___ ___ ___   ___ ___   ___ ___ ___
26 13 23   15 12 12 16   26 7   7   19 22

___ ___ ___ ___ ___ ___   ___ ___ ___   ___ ___ ___ ___   ___ ___ ___
21 18 22 15 23 8   21 12 9   7   19 22 2   26 9   22

___ ___ ___ ___ ___ ___ ___   ___ ___ ___ ___ ___   ___ ___ ___
26 15 9   22 26 23 2   4   19 18 7   22   21 12 9

___ ___ ___ ___ ___ ___ ___ .
19 26 9   5   22 8   7

Key to the Code:

F	N	R	U	A	G	O	S	V	C	H	T	D	I	E	B	W	K	Y	P	M	L	J
21	13	9	6	26	20	12	8	5	24	19	7	23	18	22	4	16	2	11	25	14	15	17

"Fruits Of Our Labor": Crafts

- Jacob's Well - Use a small Dixie cup, gray or brown paint, mosaic tiles, and some glue. Paint the cup and let it dry. Glue the mosaic "stones" all over the cup to make a well. Fill it half full with water. Tell someone the story of the woman at the well and how Jesus offered her living water.

- Ripe Harvest picture - In John 4:35, Jesus told his disciples to look at the fields, they were white for harvest. He was referring to souls of people and not actual crops. Take a legal size sheet of paper, color or paint a blue sky and a field with tall plants. Glue white cotton balls all over the field. Write John 4:35 in the sky. Let the picture remind you that Jesus has given us work to do in telling others about Him.

Lesson 10: The Sermon on the Mount

Text: Matthew 5, 6 & 7

 ## "Growing In The Word": Lesson Text And Discussion

*This is a long lesson covering three full chapters. Feel free to spread this lesson out over more than one day if necessary to cover the material thoroughly.

Read Matthew 5:1-2. Where does Jesus go to teach the people? (On a mountain) How many came to listen to him? (Multitudes – that means a lot!) Jesus is about to preach one of the greatest sermons ever.

Read Matthew 5:3-12. This passage is usually called "The Beatitudes". These verses contain attitudes that we are to "be". Jesus begins all of these beatitudes with the word "blessed" which can mean "happy". In verse 3, "poor in spirit" means to be humble before God realizing our spiritual condition before Him. In verse 4, when he refers to mourning, he is referring to being sad over our sin. In verse 5, he speaks of the meek. What is meekness? (Not weakness, but rather power under control, gentleness) In verse 6, Jesus says that those who really, really want to be righteous and feast on the word of God will be happy and fulfilled people. (Remember the Samaritan woman thirsting after the living water?) Verse 7 is a reminder to be merciful to others and when you are, God will also be merciful to you. Verse 8 mentions the pure in heart. What do you think it means to be pure? (Being pure means to be free from any contamination; clean; holy) Verse 9 encourages us to be peacemakers, not ones who like to pick fights or stir things up. Verses 10-12 deal with being persecuted. Jesus says you are blessed if you're persecuted for what? (Righteousness' sake – or for doing what's right) Has that ever happened to you? Have you ever been picked on or made fun of for doing what's right? Jesus reminds us that we're not alone in that. That happened to the prophets back in the Old Testament as well. If we stand for what's right, we have a great reward in heaven. Stand strong for God!

Read Matthew 5:13-16. Jesus compares his followers to two things. What are they? (Salt and light) We use salt to season food so that it will have good flavor. If salt loses it flavor, what does Jesus say it's good for? (Nothing!) And what good is light if it's hidden and no one can see it? (None) Salt and light are being compared to our influence with people. We need to have a good influence for the Lord and let it be seen. Why do we "let our light shine"? (So people can see our good works and give glory to God for them)

Read Matthew 5:17-19. Jesus is talking here about the old law which would be the law of Moses. Jesus obeyed everything in the law (fulfilled it) and encourages followers of God to obey the commands of God.

Read Matthew 5:20-26. We all know that it's wrong to murder somebody, but Jesus also tells us that it's very wrong to be angry at someone for no good reason. We need to be careful that we don't harbor hate in our hearts. Jesus also encourages us to be peacemakers. Maybe we're not mad at anyone, but we know that someone is mad at us. We need to go talk to that person and works things out.

Read Matthew 5:27-30. When you're married to someone, you are to love only that person and be faithful to them. It is not right for you to "make eyes" at someone else if you're married or to do anything with them that only married people are to do with each other. Unfaithfulness in marriage is called adultery which is a sin. Jesus also talks about the sin of lust. What is lust? (A wrong desire) When Jesus talks about plucking out your eye or cutting off your hand, he's simply trying to make a strong point that you need to get rid of whatever might be causing you to sin. Maybe someone has a book that they shouldn't read because it has bad things in it. If it tempts them to sin, what should they do with the book? (Get rid of it!)

Read Matthew 5:31-32. Jesus gives one reason only for divorce, whereas in the Old Testament times, people were divorcing their wives for all kinds of reasons. The Lord wants us to realize the seriousness of marriage. It is a lifetime commitment.

Read Matthew 5:33-37. Jesus states that we are not to swear when we promise something. You might have heard someone say, "I swear on a stack of Bibles!" when they're trying to convince someone they're telling the truth. Jesus says we need to always be people of truth so that when we say "yes" or "no", that is what we mean. There is no need of swearing.

Read Matthew 5:38-42. In Old Testament times, it began to be said, "An eye for an eye and a tooth for a tooth", meaning whatever someone did to you could be done right back to them. Fair and square, right? Wrong! Jesus teaches something completely different. If someone slaps you on one cheek, what does Jesus say to do? (Turn the other cheek to them also – not slap them back!) He also teaches us here to be generous and kind. Give to those who need and who ask; don't be selfish. Verse 41 is where we get the phrase, "second mile service". We usually use it to mean we should go above and beyond what someone asks or expects of us, to do more than is required. That is a good thing to do, but Jesus literally meant that the people should go an extra mile distance-wise. You will learn more about that in the research project.

Read Matthew 5:43-48. Some people said it was okay to hate your enemies as long as you loved your neighbors, but is that what Jesus teaches? (No!) Jesus commands us to love our enemies, and not only that, but also to do good for them and pray for them. This is not always the easiest thing to do, is it? God sometimes requires us to do hard things. He says that it's an easy thing to love people that already love you, but everybody (even ungodly people) does that. God's people do more – love those who are not always lovable. Why does He tell us to do this? (To be perfect as our Father in heaven is perfect.) Of course, we'll never be perfect like God in the sense we'll be sinless, but we're to be perfect in the sense we're to be complete in doing the things God would have us do. Follow after Him and imitate Him in all things which includes loving our enemies.

Read Matthew 6:1-4. Have you ever known someone who likes to brag about things they've done? Jesus is warning us in these verses not to be like that. When we do good works for the Lord, we're not to do it so that everyone can see it and we're not to do it so that everyone can pat us on the back and tell us how good we are. We're to do our good works to honor God and serve Him out of love for Him.

Read Matthew 6:5-15. Jesus uses these verses to teach us how to pray. Again, we're not to pray to impress people with our words, but our prayers should come from our hearts as we talk to our Father in heaven. In verses 9-13 we have what is commonly called, The Lord's Prayer. What are some things Jesus asks for in this prayer? (Your kingdom come, Your will be done, daily bread, forgiveness of sins, deliverance from Satan) These are some of the things we too can ask God for when we pray to him. Jesus refers to God's name as "hallowed". What does that mean? (holy) We are to honor and respect the name of God and never use it lightly (vainly). In verse 15, what does Jesus say we will not receive if we aren't willing to give it ourselves? (Forgiveness) This is important to remember. If we want God to forgive us of our sins, we must be willing to forgive others and not hold grudges and hatred in our hearts.

Read Matthew 6:16-18. Fasting was a common practice in Bible times and can still be practiced today. Fasting is going without food or certain kinds of food for a specified period of time. There were different reasons for fasting; to draw closer to God, to mourn, to repent, etc. Jesus teaches that there's nothing wrong with fasting, but do it for the right reason. He warns against being like the person who brags about his good deeds or prays to impress people. Don't fast so everyone can see that you're fasting and say, "Wow! He's so spiritual!" Jesus has been emphasizing that we need to do good works but have the right motive for doing them. Many "religious" people of Jesus' day were doing "religious" things just so everyone could see how "good" they were. Jesus wants us to do good works because we love God and desire to serve Him, not to be a spiritual show-off.

Read Matthew 6:19-34. Jesus has a lot to say here about wealth and material things. First, he says there's one place where we need to lay up treasures. Where is it? (Heaven) What happens to our "treasures" here on earth if we pile them up? (Moths and rust destroy and thieves steal them) Our focus should not be on how much "stuff" we can get and keep. Pretty soon, we find that no amount is ever enough. We always want more. It can get so bad that we're like a slave to it. Jesus then tells us in verse 24 that no man can serve two masters. You can't serve God and mammon. What's mammon? (Money) So, we need to make a choice. Are we going to focus on serving God or focus on serving money and all it can buy? In verse 25, Jesus encourages us to never worry about having food to eat or clothes to wear. Why not? He goes on to say how God takes cares of the birds and feeds them and He takes care of the flowers of the fields and dresses them beautifully. Who is more important to God than birds and flowers? We are! So don't you think that God will take care of us too? Of course He will! Isn't it wonderful to know that? We <u>never</u> have to worry and fret about having the things that we need. God will always provide. Verse 33 assures us that if we put God first in our life and serve Him, He will add the things we need to our lives. One thing to remember here – there is a difference between needs and wants. It doesn't say God will provide an Xbox or flat screen TV. Those are not things we need. God will always make sure we are fed and clothed; that is all we really need.

Read Matthew 7:1-6. It's usually a lot easier to point out what everyone else is doing wrong than it is to look at ourselves and admit our own mistakes. This is what Jesus warns against here. Don't go around judging everybody (pointing out everything they do wrong) and then refuse to admit what you need to correct in your own life. This doesn't mean that you can't point out *anything* that's wrong. If your friend tells a lie, you need to talk to him about it because lying is wrong. Jesus is talking about people who are always being critical and judgmental and then act like they're perfect themselves. That is not the right attitude and behavior to have.

Read Matthew 7:7-11. Jesus encourages us to "ask, seek and knock". Who are we to ask? (Our Father in heaven) Does God like to give us good things? (Of course!) When a parent loves his child, does that parent enjoy giving good gifts to his child? (Absolutely!) How wonderful it is to know that God, our Father in heaven, *wants* to give good things to us, His children, if we'll just ask Him.

Read Matthew 7:12. This verse is known as the "golden rule". What does it say? ("Whatever you want men to do to you, do also to them.") We're to treat other people the way we want to be treated, not as we think they deserve to be treated. Be proactive in treating people the right way instead of reacting to how they treat us.

Read Matthew 7:13-14. There are two paths in life. One is broad or wide and a lot of people follow that path. The other path is narrow and only a few find it. Where do the two paths lead? (The broad path leads to destruction, the narrow path leads to life – eternal life with God). Jesus is making the point that people have a choice whether they want to follow God or not. Most people, sadly, choose not to and their path leads away from God to destruction. Let's choose to follow the path that leads to God.

Read Matthew 7:15-20. Some people act like they're Christians and some even claim to be preachers, but not all of them teach the truth of God's Word. How can we tell whether someone is a false teacher or not? Jesus says, "You will know them by their fruits." What do you think he means by that? As Jesus said, have you ever seen a thornbush have grapes on it or thistle plants with figs? If a tree is good, it bears good fruit and if a tree is bad it will bear bad fruit. Look at how a person acts, what they say, and how they serve the Lord. Is it good and true or is it false? The "fruit" in their life will show you what kind of person they are.

Read Matthew 7:21-23. This passage is one we need to pay close attention to. Who does Jesus say will enter the kingdom of heaven? (The one who does the will of God) Jesus says that there will be many who *think* they're going to heaven – they believe in God, do lots of good works in His name, but they fail to do exactly what God says. We can't pick and choose things in the Bible to obey and then ignore things we don't like and think that it is okay; it's not. God requires total obedience to His will.

Read Matthew 7:24-27. Jesus ends his great sermon with a story that is now probably very familiar to us. It is the parable of the wise builder and foolish builder. Have you ever sung the song, "The wise man built his house upon the rock"? This is that story! Notice that there are two men and they both build a house. One builds on a rock. What does the other man build his house on? (Sand) Then what happens? (Storms! Rains, winds, and flood) Whose house is still standing afterward? (The wise man who built his house on the rock) Have you ever been to the beach and walked on sand? What does it do under your feet? It moves or shifts, doesn't it? Can you imagine building a house on sand? Sand is not solid and would not provide a good foundation for a house. That is why the man who built his house on the sand is called foolish. Is Jesus giving building advice here or is he speaking of something else? He's speaking of building our lives on a solid foundation and not one that moves underneath us and collapses at the first bad storm in our life. God is often called our rock in the scriptures.

He does not move; He is solid and dependable. If we build our lives on Him, will storms destroy us? No! After hard times come, we will still be standing because we depend on God.

Read Matthew 7:28-29. Jesus finishes his sermon. What is the reaction of the people? (They're astonished or surprised at his teaching.) They're surprised because he was teaching them with authority. Remember, he is just beginning his ministry and some people are probably hearing him for the first time and don't realize who he is. He's teaching them with authority by commanding them to do certain things and not do others. For example, telling them to love their enemies, turn the other cheek, etc. He has given them a lot to think about. Jesus gives us a lot to think about in this sermon as well. There are many things in it that we need to work hard on so that we can be obedient and pleasing to God. Are you up to the challenge?

Review Questions: (Answers are in the Answer Key.)

1. Where did Jesus go to preach to the people?

2. In the beatitudes, what will the merciful obtain?

3. What two things does Jesus compare our influence with?

4. Is it okay to swear?

5. What should we do for our enemies?

6. Are we supposed to do good deeds so that everyone will notice and praise us?

7. What does "hallowed" mean?

8. If we aren't willing to forgive others, what will God not do for us?

9. Where are we to lay up treasures?

10. Does Jesus want us to worry about what we'll eat or what we'll wear?

11. Whom does God feed and clothe that are of less importance than we are?

12. What rich king was not dressed as beautifully as the lilies?

13. What will God give us if we seek Him first?

14. What kind of gifts does God want to give us?

15. What does He want us to do first?

16. What does the Golden Rule say?

17. How can we tell if someone is a false teacher?

18. Whom does Jesus say will enter the kingdom of heaven?

19. Why did the wise man's house remain standing after the storm?

20. How did the people react to the sermon of Jesus?

 "Putting Down Roots": Memory Work

- Memorize the Beatitudes - Matthew 5:3-10
- Memorize Matthew 5:16
- Memorize the Lord's Prayer - Matthew 6:9-13
- Memorize Matthew 7:12

 "Farther Afield": Map Work

- There are no new mapping activities for this lesson. You could take some time to review where the regions of Galilee, Samaria, and Judea are and what major cities are located within them.

 "Harvest Fun": Games And Activities

- Sword Drill – The Bible is referred to as the "Sword of the Spirit" in Ephesians 6:17. Just as a good soldier was skilled at using his sword, so we must be skilled in using God's Word. Let's practice finding scriptures! Each person will need their Bible. See how quickly you can locate the following verses from the sermon on the mount. After one person reads a verse aloud, let everyone search their Bible in Matthew 5, 6 & 7 to locate the verse. Give everyone a chance to find it. Answers are in the Answer Key.

1. "Blessed are the peacemakers, for they shall be called sons of God."

2. "Judge not, that you be not judged."

3. "Give us this day our daily bread."

4. "Do not lay up for yourselves treasures on earth, where moth and rust destroy and where thieves break in and steal."

5. "Let your light so shine before men, that they may see your good works and glorify your Father in heaven."

6. "Therefore, whatever you want men to do to you, do also to them."

7. "Our Father in heaven, hallowed be Your name."

8. "And whoever compels you to go one mile, go with him two."

9. "But seek you first the kingdom of God and His righteousness and all these things shall be added unto you."

10. "Ask, and it will be given to you; seek, and you will find; knock, and it will be opened to you."

• "What did Jesus say about..." - For this activity, you will need index cards. Write the following words, one per card, and place them in a stack on the table, face down. Words to write: peacemakers, persecution, salt, light, anger, adultery, divorce, swearing, sharing, love, doing good deeds, prayer, forgiveness, fasting, money, worry, judging, asking, golden rule, false teachers, eternal life, building. Let a player pick a card and read the word aloud. They should then try to recite a verse or talk about what Jesus said about the subject from the sermon on the mount. If the player can't think of anything, go to the next player to answer and so on until the subject on the card has been explained by someone. Then pick the next card and continue. This serves as a review activity of the lessons Jesus was teaching the people then and to us today.

"Digging Deeper": Research

• Second Mile – We often hear it said about Christian service that we should "go the second mile". This comes from what Jesus taught in Matthew 5:41. We use it in the sense that we should be willing to do extra things for people, to go above and beyond and that is a good thing to do, but Jesus was literally teaching the people to go an extra mile – distance wise! What did he mean by this? Research the Roman law concerning this.

- Jewish Synagogues – In Matthew 6, Jesus mentions the synagogues. What were they for and when and how did they come into being?

 "Food For Thought": Puzzles

- Matching – Match the beginning of the verse on the left to the rest of it on the right. Answers are in the Answer Key.

1. Blessed are the pure in heart...	who asks you.
2. You are the salt...	you will know them.
3. Let your light so shine...	how they grow.
4. Your kingdom come...	before men.
5. Give to him...	for they shall see God.
6. Consider the lilies of the field...	that you be not judged.
7. Seek first the kingdom of God and...	of the earth.
8. Whatever you want men to do to you...	your will be done.
9. Judge not...	all these things will be added to you.
10. By their fruits...	do also to them.

- Matching #2 – Match the verse on the left with its reference (where it's found) on the right. Answers are in the Answer Key.

1. Our Father in heaven, hallowed be Your name.	Matthew 5:48
2. Which of you by worrying can add one cubit to his stature?	Matthew 5:12
3. Or if he asks a fish, will he give him a serpent?	Matthew 6:11
4. The people were astonished at his teaching.	Matthew 6:24
5. Rejoice and be exceedingly glad, for great is your reward...	Matthew 7:10
6. You are the light of the world.	Matthew 5:14
7. Give us this day our daily bread.	Matthew 6:9
8. No one can serve two masters.	Matthew 6:27
9. Whoever compels you to go one, go with him two.	Matthew 7:28
10. You shall be perfect, as your Father in heaven is perfect.	Matthew 5:41

"Fruits Of Our Labor": Crafts

- Illustrate a teaching of Jesus – Pick a lesson from the Sermon on the Mount such as the Golden Rule, Wise Man/Foolish Man, loving your enemies, laying up treasure in heaven, etc. and make an illustration of it. Copy the verse or verses that your picture comes from onto the picture itself.

- Beatitudes Book – The beatitudes in Matthew chapter 5 are attitudes that we should "be". Make a small book to remind you of each one. You will need 3- 8 ½ by 11-inch white pieces of paper, scissors, crayons or colored pencils, ruler, hole punch and yarn. First, take the 3 pieces of paper and fold each one in half from top edge to bottom edge, then in half again from left edge to right edge. Open them back up. Cut each piece of paper in half along the middle scored line horizontally. Stack all of the cut pieces together to form a booklet. (You will not need one piece.) You should now have 5 - 8 ½ inch wide folded pieces nested together. Close the booklet and punch three holes along the folded edge about ½ inch from the top, ½ inch from the bottom and one hole in the middle. Each hole should measure about ½ inch in from the folded edge. If you'd like, you can use colored foam pieces to serve as a front and back cover for your book. Just measure each piece about 1/4" bigger all the way around than your paper and mark and punch three holes to align with your pages. Thread pieces of yarn through each hole and tie securely to hold your book together. Now you are ready to write! On the front cover write, "The Beatitudes" . As you open the first page, on the left-hand page, draw a picture or use stickers to illustrate Matthew 5:3. On the right-hand page, write out the verse. For example, to be poor in spirit means to realize how much we need God and how empty we are without Him. To illustrate it, you might draw an empty jar. For "those who mourn" you could draw tears. For "Blessed are the meek", draw something that represents gentleness. Each open-fold page gets a picture on the left side and the verse written on the right. There will be 8 beatitudes in all (verses 3-10). Be creative with this and use it to remind you of the way God wants you to be!

Lesson 11: Jesus Heals a Paralytic

Text: Luke 5:16-26

"Growing In The Word": Lesson Text And Discussion

*This event can also be found in Matthew 9:1-8 and Mark 2:1-12.

Read Luke 5:16. This is a short verse, but one that can still teach us something important. Why would Jesus often go off by himself ? (To pray) Jesus realized the value of prayer and so should we. Let's make sure we take time to be in a quiet place so we can spend time in prayer with God.

Read Luke 5:17. We learn from Mark 2:1 that Jesus is in the city of Capernaum. What is he doing and who are some of the people around him? (He's teaching. Some of the people gathered are Pharisees and teachers of the law.) This verse also lets us know that Jesus was healing people.

Read Luke 5:18-19. There is a man who is a paralytic which means he cannot walk. He is carried on a bed by some men to the house where Jesus is teaching and healing. Why don't they go in? (It is too crowded.) What might someone in that situation be tempted to do? He might just think, "Oh, it's hopeless. There's so many people here that I'll never get to Jesus. What's the use – I'll just go back home." But that is not what this man thinks! He's determined to see Jesus and will do whatever it takes to reach him. What faith! Not only does the paralytic have faith, but also the men who are carrying him as they help him reach his goal. Not to be outdone by the crowd, they find another way. Where do they go? (Up on the roof) How do they get the man lying on his bed to Jesus? (They remove part of the roof tiles and lower the bed down into the house.)

Read Luke 5:20. What does Jesus see? (Their faith) What is faith? Faith is believing in God, but it is also more than that. It is taking God at His word. You believe not only in Him, but in everything He's done and says He will do. This man and his friends believe in Jesus and in what he can do for this paralytic. Jesus sees this immediately. What does he say first? ("Man, your sins are forgiven you.") Why do think Jesus says this? Not only is Jesus the healer of physical bodies, but he is the healer of spiritual sickness as well. Man's real problem is sin and Jesus has the cure for it!

Read Luke 5:21. The scribes and Pharisees are Jewish religious leaders who are well educated in the Jewish religious law (law of Moses). They start talking among themselves and getting upset. What are they upset about? (Jesus telling the man his sins are forgiven when only God can forgive sin) What do they not believe about Jesus? (They do not believe that he is the Messiah, the Son of God.) If they did believe, they wouldn't have any problem with him forgiving sin. They say to each other that he is speaking blasphemies. What do you think blasphemy is? Blasphemy is being hateful and irreverent to God; it is saying God can't do something that He can, or saying He's doing something that He would never do (something that is wrong). For example, calling God a liar; it is irreverent and it is something God would never do. These religious leaders are accusing Jesus of being irreverent to God by acting like he himself is God by forgiving the paralytic's sins.

Read Luke 5:22-24. Jesus knows exactly what they're thinking. How does he know? (Because he's the Son of God!) Then he asks them a question. What does he ask them? (Which is easier, to say, 'Your sins are forgiven', or to say, 'Rise up and walk'?) Now which one would be easier for the scribes and Pharisees to do? Neither! They cannot forgive someone's sins, nor can they make a paralyzed man walk again – but Jesus can! He is going to now show them a confirmation that what he said ("Man, your sins are forgiven") was right. He is going to perform a miracle. Remember what the purpose of miracles is? To confirm the Word (show the word of God to be true). What does Jesus now say to the paralytic? ("Arise, take up your bed, and go to your house.")

Read Luke 5:25-26. How long did it take the paralyzed man to get up? He got up immediately! What did he do next? (He took up his bed and went home, praising God.) If you were that man, how would you feel? Would you be amazed, in shock, happy? Just think what a day this man had – he woke up paralyzed, went to see Jesus, was told his sins were forgiven, and then was healed so he could walk again. Amazing! No wonder he glorified God all the way home. He *knew* who Jesus was and what he could do for him. This man had faith. What was the reaction of all the people who were there? (They were amazed, they glorified God, they were filled with fear.) The people who witnessed this event give the praise and glory to God as is right. Always remember to give God the glory and praise for the wonderful things He does in your life too!

Review Questions: (Answers are in the Answer Key.)

1. What city did this likely take place in?

2. Who was at the house with Jesus?

3. What was Jesus doing for the people?

4. Why couldn't the paralyzed man get to Jesus?

5. How did the paralytic's friends get him into the house?

6. What is the first thing Jesus said to him?

7. What did the scribes and Pharisees think Jesus was doing?

8. What did Jesus tell the paralytic to do?

9. How long did it take the man to get up from his bed?

10. What did he do as he went home?

11. What did Jesus see that the paralytic and his friends had?

12. What is the purpose of miracles?

13. What was the crowd's reaction to this event?

"Putting Down Roots": Memory Work

- Memorize Matthew 9:2

- Memorize Luke 5:24, 25

"Farther Afield": Map Work

Map 1

- There is nothing new to mark in this lesson, but look at your maps and reacquaint yourself as to the locations of the region of Galilee, the region of Judea, the city of Jerusalem, and the city of Capernaum. Capernaum (according to Mark 2:1) is probably where this event occurred. Which region is it located in? How far is it from Jesus' home base of Nazareth?

"Harvest Fun": Games And Activities

- Act it Out – This is a great story to act out if you have enough people. (Just be careful with the guy on the bed!) If there's only two of you, one can be Jesus and the other the paralytic lying on his bed at Jesus' feet. Recite the words Jesus spoke to him and act out the man's reaction to what Jesus said. Don't forget he glorified God all the way home. This man was so happy because he had seen Jesus who had healed him spiritually and physically.

- "Arise, and take up your bed!" Race – For two players, you will need two pillows, two sleeping bags or blankets, and string or twine to tie the beds up. Before you begin, let each player lay their sleeping bag out on the floor with their pillow on it and lay down on their bed. When "Go" is called, each player will race to "Arise, and take up their bed!" by rolling up their sleeping bag with the pillow tucked inside, tie it up with string or twine, then race to a designated finish line first. If playing this game with two teams, play it relay style by letting a player race to a designated point with the bed roll, unrolling the bed and placing the pillow down on it, then racing back to tag the next player on their team to run down and roll it up, racing it back to the next member of their team and so on rolling and unrolling the bed until the team that finishes first is the winner. When Jesus healed the paralytic, he immediately arose and took up his bed just as Jesus instructed him. He was healed from being paralyzed instantly!

"Digging Deeper": Research

- Houses in Bible times – What would a typical Jewish home look like? What kind of roof would it have? How would the men have carried the paralytic up to the rooftop? Draw an illustration of a Jewish home from what you learn or print out a picture.

- "Son of Man" - Jesus refers to himself as the "Son of Man" in Luke 5:24. What does that name mean? What Old Testament prophecy does it come from? How many times in the New Testament is Jesus referred to in this way?

"Food For Thought": Puzzles

- Word Scramble – Unscramble the following words from the lesson. Answers are in the Answer Key.

y r d a p e	_____	t i f a h	_____
g t a h c i e n	_____	s h e m p b a l i s e	_____
e s r h i p a e s	_____	a s t h e r	_____
r o w e p	_____	r s e i a	_____
d c w r o	_____	k a l w	_____
p e s t o u h o	_____	g n r t a e s	_____

- Word Search Puzzle – Answers are in the Answer Key.

```
E R A A A P H A R I S E E S S S
S P T G M E C O L E C R O W D O
U U K S A A O D S S E H S O O N
O R S L R F Z E E D Y S G N A O
H G I E A S S E N E V I G R O F
N N A D J W I L D E R N E S S M
G N I Y F I R O L G T S R I O A
S D H F C I T Y L A R A P I H N
```

wilderness	Pharisees	healing	paralytic
crowd	house	roof	sins
forgiveness	Son of Man	walk	glorifying
Jesus	God	amazed	

 ## "Fruits Of Our Labor": Crafts

- Paralytic on his bed – For this craft, you will need 2 popsicle sticks, scrap fabric, craft glue, a pipe cleaner, wooden clothespin with solid round head, and a sharpie. Use the clothespin for the paralytic man. Draw a face on the round head with a sharpie and hair on top if you like. Next, wrap the body with scrap fabric and secure with a couple dots of glue. Take a 4-inch piece of pipe cleaner and wrap it once or twice around the neck to secure it leaving an even length on each side folded down toward the body for arms. Now take another piece of fabric that is 4 inches long by 5 inches wide. Lay it flat with the wrong side of the fabric facing up. Lay each popsicle stick about ¼ inch in from each edge. Glue them to the fabric and let dry. Then roll the popsicle sticks toward each other a couple of times and secure with a few dots of glue. Let dry then turn it over and lay the paralytic on his bed. You may want to use this for the next craft.

- Use Lego's or building blocks to build the house where Jesus was with the crowd. Make sure you're able to remove a part of the roof for the paralytic man to be lowered through. Use action figures, Lego people, or pipe cleaner stick figures to recreate the scene from the story. Video the story or show someone the story by using the props you've made and tell the story as you move the pieces around to act it out. Don't forget when the paralytic man is healed, he takes up his bed and heads home glorifying God. Roll up the bed you made in the first craft, then bend his pipe cleaner arm to hold it as he walks home.

Lesson 12: Jesus Calms the Storm

Text: Mark 4:35-41

 ## "Growing In The Word": Lesson Text And Discussion

*Matthew 8:23-27 and Luke 8:22-25 also record this event.

Read Mark 4:35. What time of day was it? (Evening) Jesus had been teaching the people in parables during the day while sitting in a boat and now he and his disciples are going to cross the Sea of Galilee. Back in verse 1 of this chapter, it tells us the reason why Jesus was teaching the people from a boat. What was the reason? (The crowd was so great that Jesus got into a boat to face them and allow more people to see and hear him.)

Read Mark 4:36. Is the boat that Jesus and his disciples are in the only one on the water? (No) The Bible says there were other little boats that were with him too. It's possible that while Jesus was teaching the people from the boat, some people went out in their own little boats to hear him, or were already out in the water fishing and came near to hear him. So, he would have had an audience on the land and sea.

Read Mark 4:37. What happened and how did it affect the boat? (A great storm came up and the waves started filling the boat.) Do you like storms? Some people like to hear the rain, but when it gets very windy and the lightning flashes and the thunder cracks and booms loudly in the sky, it can make many people afraid. How afraid would you be if you were out on a lake in a small boat in the middle of a really bad storm and then your boat started filling up with water? What would you think might happen? How do you think the disciples feel right now?

Read Mark 4:38. What is Jesus doing during all of this? (He's sleeping on a pillow in the stern which is the back of the boat.) Do you think you could sleep in that boat during such a terrible storm? Why do you think he could peacefully sleep through that? Jesus was not afraid of any storm because he is the one in control. That should be a comfort for us and something to always remember. God is always in control so we never have to be afraid of what's going to happen. Psalm 56:3 reminds us what to do when we're afraid: "*Whenever I am afraid, I will trust in You.*" Is this what his disciples were doing? Were they trusting in Jesus? (No) They woke him up and asked him a question. What was it? ("Do you not care that we are perishing?") In other words, they're saying, "We're going to die and you just lay there sleeping! How could you?" They're upset because they're afraid.

Read Mark 4:39. What did Jesus do in response? (He got up and rebuked, or scolded, the wind and the sea.) Jesus said, "Peace be still!" to the wind and the waves and they obeyed him! How is it that Jesus can command the wind and the sea? He is the creator of those things and the master of them. Remember, he is in control!

Read Mark 4:40. Jesus asked them two questions. What were they? (1. "Why are you so fearful?" 2. "How is it that you have no faith?") It would be natural to have some fear in this situation so why do you think Jesus is asking them why they are afraid? The answer is in his second question. If they had faith in him and who he is, then they shouldn't be afraid because he is with them.

Read Mark 4:41. What effect did this have on the disciples in the boat? (They were afraid at what he had done and wondering about him.) They were amazed at seeing him display so much power that he could command the weather. Just as they were amazed, we too can be amazed as we read of the wonderful power of our awesome Lord and Savior!

Review Questions: (Answers are in the Answer Key.)

1. What time of day did this occur?

2. What is Jesus sitting in?

3. What had he been doing all day?

4. Who was with him?

5. What arose?

6. What was Jesus doing while this was going on?

7. How did his disciples feel about that?

8. What did Jesus say to the wind and the waves?

9. What effect did this have on the weather?

10. What two things did Jesus ask his disciples?

11. What was their reaction to this miracle?

12. What did they say obeyed Jesus?

 ## "Putting Down Roots": Memory Work

- Memorize Matthew 8:27

- Memorize Mark 4:39

- Memorize Psalm 56:3

"Farther Afield": Map Work

Map 1

- Locate the Sea of Galilee – This is the body of water that Jesus was crossing in the boat. What are some other names for it?

 ## "Harvest Fun": Games And Activities

- "Peace be still!" - This game is to be played like red light, green light. You will need to play this in a yard or long room. Choose one person to be Jesus. This person will lay down on a pillow, at one end of the yard or room, pretending to be asleep like Jesus was in the boat. The other players will start at the other end of the yard or room. As long as Jesus is "sleeping", the other players can move forward acting like blowing wind or crashing waves, making lots of noise. As soon as "Jesus" stands up and says, "Peace be still!", everyone freezes and remains frozen and silent until he lays back down. The game continues until someone finally reaches the "sleeping Jesus" and tags him. Then they can pretend to be Jesus next.

- Tell a Bible story – Use index cards and draw one picture per card to use for this game. Draw a picture of these items from the lesson, one per card: pillow, boat, crowd of people, storm, wind, faith, sea, someone sleeping, Jesus. If you have trouble drawing something, you may write the word on the card. Shuffle the cards and place them face down on a table. Let one person draw the top card and lay it face up for everyone to see. That person will start by telling a Bible story about the item. It can be any Bible story. The person to the left then tells a different Bible story still using the same item, and so on around the table until one person fails to come up with a Bible story that hasn't been mentioned yet. That person is then out. For example, the card has a picture of a sun on it. The first person may tell the story of how the sun stood still for the Israelites during a battle, the next person may tell the story of the fourth day of creation when God made the sun, moon and stars, and the next person may tell the story of Joseph's dream of the sun, moon, and stars bowing down to him. If the next person can't think of a different story to tell about the sun, he's out. The next person picks the top card and places it face up on the table and play continues as before until only one person is left. That person is the winner!

"Digging Deeper": Research

- Boats in the Bible – Research what boats and small fishing vessels looked like in the time of Jesus. Would you feel safe in a bad storm if you were in a boat like that? Now you can have a picture of the boat in your head whenever you read this story.

- God of nature – Jesus commanded the wind and the sea and they obeyed him. Look up these passages to learn more about God as the creator of nature, how He controls it, and how He uses things in nature for His purposes.

  Psalm 33:6-9; Colossians 1:16; Psalm 65:9-13; Psalm 147:7-9, 12-18; Jeremiah 10:13; Psalm 29:3; Job 37:2-13; Psalm 114:1-8; Joshua 10:9-11; Psalm 98:4-9

 ## "Food For Thought": Puzzles

- Coded Message -

___ ___ ___ ___   ___ ___ ___   ___ ___ ___ ___   ___ ___   ___ ___ ___ ___
4   19 12   24 26 13   7   19 18 8   25 22   7   19 26 7

___ ___ ___ ___   ___ ___ ___   ___ ___ ___ ___   ___ ___ ___
22 5   22 13   7   19 22   4   18 13 23   26 13 23

___ ___ ___   ___ ___ ___   ___ ___ ___ ___   ___ ___ ___ ?
7   19 22   8   22 26   12 25 22 2   19 18 14

Key to the Code:

F	N	R	U	A	G	O	S	V	C	H	T	D	I	E	B	W	K	Y	P	M	L	J
21	13	9	6	26	20	12	8	5	24	19	7	23	18	22	25	4	16	2	11	14	15	17

• Crossword Puzzle – Answers are in the Answer Key.

Across

2 Jesus had been sitting in this all day
4 What Jesus had just left behind
7 Time of day when this event happened
9 Jesus said to the wind, " _____ be still"
10 What Jesus was laying on
12 What Jesus was doing during the storm

Down

1 What the disciples did not have
3 Part of the boat Jesus was in
5 Name the disciples called him
6 They feared
8 _____ These beat into the boat
11 "Even the wind and sea _____ him"

"Fruits Of Our Labor": Crafts

- Making Waves – Have some fun tossing a boat around in the waves! You will need a large, clear heavy-duty ziploc bag, a large bottle of blue hair gel, some small plastic fish and a boat. To make the boat, draw and color a picture of a boat on heavy paper like card stock. (Don't make it too big!) Cut it out and laminate it or cover it completely with contact paper so that it's sealed from moisture. Place a few small plastic fish (optional) and the boat into the plastic bag. Squirt in the hair gel. Squeeze out as much air from the bag as you can, then seal it tight. You may want to tape the bag shut with packing tape or duct tape so it doesn't leak. Lay your bag on a flat surface and "squish" it around with your hands to toss the boat in the waves.

- Cake Decorating – You will need a cake mix, two tubs of vanilla frosting, plus blue food coloring, goldfish crackers (optional), and a few graham crackers. Bake the cake according to the package instructions in two square pans or two round pans and let it cool. Frost the top of one layer and place the second layer on top of the first layer. Tint some vanilla frosting light blue and spread it over the entire cake. Use the back of a spoon to push slightly into the frosting and up to make waves. If you'd like, place some goldfish crackers on top of the cake and push some into the sides of the cake. To make a boat: take one graham cracker and break it in half. Stand it on its side and push into the middle of the top of the cake. This will be the back of your boat. Take two more graham crackers and place them against either edge of the "back", standing them on their sides and pushing them slightly down into the frosting. These are the sides of your boat. Take another graham cracker and break it in half. Place these against the edges of the "sides" and touch them together to form a "V" shape at the bow, or front, of the boat. Your boat should now be formed. If you'd like you can tint a small amount of the frosting brown to frost the boat or leave it brown as is from the crackers. Now show your cake off, tell the story of Jesus calming the storm from the boat, then eat your creation!

Lesson 13: Feeding the Five Thousand and Jesus Walks on the Water

Text: Mark 6:32-44; Matthew 14:22-33

 "Growing In The Word": Lesson Text And Discussion

*These two events may also be found in Matthew 14:13-21; Luke 9:11-17; John 6:1-14 (Feeding the five thousand) and Mark 6:45-51; John 6:15-21 (Jesus walks on the water)

Read Mark 6:32-33. From the previous verses in this chapter, we learn that Jesus had sent his apostles out to do works that Jesus had commanded them and now they're gathering back together to tell him all they've done. They are all tired and had not had time to eat that day so they decide to go off by themselves to take a break. Where do they go? (A deserted place) How do they get there? (By boat) They had a good plan, but it didn't work. The crowd saw them leaving and knew where they were heading. What did the people do? (Ran ahead to meet Jesus and his disciples when they landed)

Read Mark 6:34. They land the boat and Jesus sees the crowds of people. Is he upset? (No) The Bible says he was "moved with compassion". What does that mean? He felt kind and loving toward the people and wanted to give them what they needed. What did they seem like to him? (Sheep without a shepherd) He saw that they needed guidance, direction, instruction, care. What does he begin to do? (Teach them)

Read Mark 6:35-36. The disciples start to get concerned because it's late. Since they're in a deserted place, the disciples want Jesus to send the people away to the villages to do what? (Buy bread – it's dinner time!)

Read Mark 6:37. What does Jesus tell them to do? (Give them something to eat) Can you imagine the disciples' reaction? There are thousands of people out there! What do they think they'll have to do which would be impossible for them? (Go and buy food for everyone) How much do you think it would cost today if you had to go to the store and buy food for over 5,000 people? It would be a lot of money! How much money do the disciples think it will cost them? (200 hundred denarii – which they don't have!) This was a large sum of money back then and it still wouldn't have been enough to buy sufficient food.

Read Mark 6:38. Jesus asks them what food is available. We learn from John 6:9 that there is a little boy in the crowd who has five loaves of bread and two fish. He is willing to share his food, but that's not going to be quite enough, is it?

Read Mark 6:39-41. What does Jesus command them to do? (Sit down in groups) He then takes the food that the boy shared, looks up to heaven and...? (Blesses the food or prays over it) He starts to divide it up and hand it to the disciples to distribute. How many people received food? (All)

Read Mark 6:42-44. Did anyone go hungry? (No) Not only was everyone fed, but there was food left over. How much food was left? (12 baskets full!) Verse 44 says there were about 5,000 men. Women and children would have been extra so the total number of people fed would have been much greater than 5,000!

Read Matthew 14:22-23. This event happens right after the feeding of the 5,000. Remember that Jesus and the disciples were already worn out before the feeding event so they are probably really tired now. What did Jesus tell the disciples to do? (Get into the boat to sail to the other side of the lake.) What did Jesus do in the meantime? (Sent the crowds away) Now the disciples have put out to sea, but Jesus is still on land. Where does he go and why? (To a mountain to pray)

Read Matthew 14:24-25. It's now night and the disciples' boat is in the middle of the sea. Jesus is still on land at the shore. What does he see? (The boat is being tossed by the waves because a strong wind had come up.) Jesus then does something amazing – he starts walking on the water out toward the boat!

Read Matthew 14:26-27. When the disciples see him, they're scared. What do they think they're seeing? (A ghost) Remember, it's at night so it's dark. The wind is blowing hard, waves are probably splashing up around them and then they see a figure of a man coming toward them on the water. Most likely, Jesus is dressed in white or a light color since that was the color of clothing that poorer people wore. No wonder they think he's a ghost! What does Jesus say to them as he approaches? ("It is I; don't be afraid.") This is similar to what he said when he calmed the storm. He wants them to realize that they never have to be afraid when he is with them. Jesus is always with us too which means he can calm our fears when we're tempted to feel afraid.

Read Matthew 14:28-29. Who wanted to get out of the boat to come to Jesus? (Peter) Jesus says, "Come", and Peter starts to walk on the water himself! Can you imagine what that must have been like?

Read Matthew 14:30-31. Peter starts off pretty good, but then something goes wrong and he begins to sink. When he first got out of the boat, he's looking toward Jesus. As he's walking on the water, he takes his eyes off of Jesus and instead starts looking at the stormy winds blowing and the waves crashing and he begins to be afraid. That is also when he begins to sink. In his panic and fear, what does he cry out? ("Lord, save me!") What does Jesus do? (Reaches out his hand and pulls him up to safety) Jesus asks him why he had so little faith, and why did he doubt? We get into the same trouble today if we take our eyes off of Jesus and focus instead on all of the bad things and trouble around us. It can make us doubt or be afraid and it weakens our faith. The lesson is to keep our eyes on Jesus!

Read Matthew 14:32-33. What happened when Jesus got into the boat? (The wind ceased) The disciples are amazed and say to Jesus, "Truly, You are the Son of God." Amen!

Review Questions: (Answers are in the Answer Key.)

1. What was Jesus moved with when he saw the multitudes?

2. What kind of place were they in?

3. What did the people need because of the time of day?

4. What was the disciples' solution to the problem?

5. What did Jesus tell the disciples to do?

6. How much did the disciples think it was going to cost?

7. Did the disciples have this amount?

8. Who had some food to share?

9. How much food did he have?

10. What did Jesus command everyone to do?

11. What did Jesus do before he passed the food out to the people?

12. Did everyone get something to eat?

13. How much food was leftover?

14. How many were fed by Jesus?

15. When the disciples got into their boat, where did Jesus go and why?

16. What difficulty did the disciples run into out in the middle of the sea?

17. Jesus saw their difficulty and did what?

18. What did the disciples think they were seeing?

19. What did Jesus say to them?

20. Who asked to come to Jesus on the water?

21. What happened to him and why?

22. What did Jesus do?

23. What happened when Jesus got in the boat?

24. What did the disciples call Jesus?

"Putting Down Roots": Memory Work

- Memorize Matthew 14:33

- Memorize Mark 6:34

- Memorize Luke 9:16, 17

 ## "Farther Afield": Map Work

Map 3

- Locate the Sea of Tiberius

- Locate the city of Tiberius

- Locate the city of Bethsaida and find the deserted place or area outside of the city. You may want to mark it with a little fish symbol to remind you of this event.

- Study a good map of the Sea of Galilee and all of the cities dotted along its shore. You will see why Jesus and the disciples were crossing the sea, or lake, so many times as they traveled from city to city. Find out how many miles across this sea is. Would it have taken long for them to cross it?

 ## "Harvest Fun": Games And Activities

- Pictionary Review – This game will help review all 13 lessons covered in this book. To play this game you will need a white board, chalkboard, or clipboard with drawing paper and something to draw with. You will need to make cards with the names of people, places, events, or things from the Bible stories – one item per card. Have someone who is not playing the game write the cards up. When everything is prepared, divide up into 2 teams. Let a player pick a card, making sure no one else sees it. He then has one minute to draw what's on the card. Only his team may guess. If they guess correctly what it is <u>and</u> what story it's from, they get a point. If they don't guess correctly, the other team has a chance to guess and get the point. Play continues until all the cards are used. The team with the highest score wins. (*It is possible that some cards will apply to more than one Bible story. A point may be awarded as long as a Bible story is identified correctly.) Items to be written on the cards: tax collector, fig tree, angel, dove, river, locusts, temple, manger, shepherds, mountain, boat, fish, loaves of bread, storm, house, well, stones, gold, Mary, dream, King Herod, wise men, wine, wedding, pillow, waterpot, paralytic man

"Digging Deeper": Research

- Denarius – This was a denomination of money in Bible times. Was this a common coin during Jesus' day? What was it used for? What did it look like? How much was it worth? How much would 200 denarii be worth? Would it have been enough money to buy bread for over 5,000 people?

- Barley loaves – The five loaves of bread that the little boy shared were barley loaves. (John 6:9) What was the significance of barley? Who usually ate it? When was it harvested? Who else besides Jesus multiplied loaves of barley to feed many people?

"Food For Thought": Puzzles

- Who Am I/What Am I? - Guess the answer after reading the following clues. All of the answers pertain to this lesson. Answers are in the Answer Key.

1. I am a useful container for carrying things. _____

2. I am equal to a day's wages and am useful for buying things. _____

3. I shared my lunch. _____

4. I was offered before anyone ate. _____

5. Some of us ran ahead to see Jesus. _____

6. Five of me were made out of barley. _____

7. I am a follower of Jesus who got out of the boat while at sea. _____

8. I'm not real, but the disciples thought they saw one of me. _____

9. I'm a bit blustery. _____

10. I am a useful vessel on water. _____

- Matching Puzzle – Fill in the blanks on the left with the letter of the correct definition on the right. Answers are in the Answer Key.

____ 1. denarius   a. wonder at something

____ 2. barley   b. Roman coin common in Jesus' day

____ 3. compassion   c. appearing empty

____ 4. fragments   d. student or follower of Jesus

____ 5. marvel   e. parts of a whole

____ 6. multitudes   f. showing distress or anxiety

____ 7. deserted   g. stop

____ 8. troubled   h. a grain used to make bread

____ 9. cease   i. pity and concern for others

____ 10. disciple   j. lots of people

 "Fruits Of Our Labor": Crafts

- Basket of bread and fish – The little boy who shared his food had a basket of five loaves of bread and two fish. You will need: a plastic pint container (like what strawberries come in), 1-inch wide strips of ribbon or fabric, modeling clay or play-doh, and glue. First, take the strips of ribbon or fabric and weave them in an over and under motion going around and around the plastic container starting at a bottom corner. Secure ends of ribbon or fabric with glue. Trim excess ribbon. Next, use modeling clay or play-doh to form five loaves of bread and two fish. Place them in your finished basket.

- Jesus Walking on Water – You will need: a small mirror (you can get little ones at a dollar store), an action figure to represent Jesus (Christian bookstores have these) or a cut-out picture of Jesus, blue tissue paper, glue, fish stickers (optional), a plastic boat, and a disposable shallow aluminum pan. Glue your figure of Jesus to the middle of the mirror (standing up) and let it dry. Take pieces of blue tissue paper and crumple them up. Spread them back out and start gluing them into the bottom of the pan, filling it up with the "sea". If you'd like, place a few fish stickers down among the waves. Nestle the plastic boat off to the side in the "waves". Then, place the mirror with Jesus on it on top of the sea.

Answer Key

ANSWER KEY

Lesson 1:

Review Questions:

1. Who told Joseph about Jesus' birth? (An angel of the Lord)

2. How did he appear to Joseph? (In a dream)

3. What did the angel tell Joseph to not be afraid to do? (Take Mary as his wife)

4. What Old Testament prophet is quoted in Matthew 1:23? (Isaiah)

5. What does Immanuel mean? (God with us)

6. What did the angel tell Joseph that Jesus would do? (Save His people from their sins)

7. Who told Mary about Jesus' birth? (The angel, Gabriel)

8. What city did Mary live in? (Nazareth)

9. What is impossible with God? (Nothing!)

10. Who was Mary's cousin? (Elizabeth)

11. What amazing news did the angel give Mary concerning her cousin? (Her cousin, Elizabeth was six months pregnant. This was amazing because she was old and past child-bearing.)

12. Mary called herself the _____ of the Lord. (Servant)

- Crossword Puzzle -

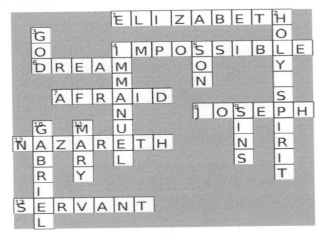

Lesson 2:

Review Questions:

1. Which Caesar ordered a census be taken? (Augustus)

2. What city did Joseph and Mary live in? (Nazareth)

3. What city did they have to travel to? (Bethlehem)

4. What did Mary wrap baby Jesus in? (Swaddling clothes)

5. What did Mary lay Jesus in? (A manger)

6. Who were out in the fields at night? (Shepherds)

7. Who appeared to them? (An angel of the Lord)

8. What was the message he gave to the shepherds? (A Savior is born)

9. After the shepherds visited Mary, Joseph, and baby Jesus, what did they do? (Told the good news to everyone they met)

10. Whom did they glorify and praise for what they had seen and heard? (God)

- Who Am I?/What Am I? - 1) manger, 2) Caesar Augustus, 3) shepherd, 4) sheep, 5) Mary, 6) Joseph, 7) inn, 8) Bethlehem, 9) swaddling cloths, 10) Nazareth

- Word Search Puzzle -

Lesson 3:

Review Questions:

1. In what city was Jesus born? (Bethlehem)

2. Who was king of Judea? (Herod)

3. Where did the wise men come from? (The East)

4. How many wise men were there? (The Bible doesn't say)

5. Why did Herod want to find Jesus? (To kill him)

6. Why did the wise men want to find him? (To worship him)

7. What led the wise men to Jesus? (A star)

8. What gifts did they give Jesus? (Gold, frankincense, and myrrh)

9. How were the wise men warned not to return to Herod? (In a dream)

10. Where was Joseph told to take Mary and Jesus? (Egypt)

11. What Old Testament prophet prophesied that Jesus would be in Egypt? (Hosea)

12. When was Joseph told it was safe to return from Egypt? (After Herod's death)

13. Where did Jesus' family go to live? (Nazareth in Galilee)

14. What wicked order did Herod issue? (To kill all the baby boys aged two and under in Bethlehem and the surrounding districts)

- Word Scramble – Bethlehem, star, gold, frankincense, Egypt, Israel, Nazareth, wise men, scribes, Herod, worship, myrrh, dream, angel, Galilee, Joseph, gifts, house

- Matching - 1) Bethlehem, 2) The East, 3) Herod, 4) Star, 5) Gold, frankincense and myrrh, 6) Dream, 7) Egypt, 8) Unknown, 9) Nazareth, 10) Judea, 11) Galilee, 12) Archelaus, 13) Three, 14) Ruler, 15) Jerusalem

Lesson 4:

Review Questions:

1. What city did Jesus live in? (Nazareth)

2. What was he filled with? (Wisdom)

3. What city did his family travel to? (Jerusalem)

4. What was the occasion? (Passover feast)

5. How old was Jesus at this time? (12)

6. Did his parents know he'd stayed behind when they started for home? (No)

7. Where was he? (In the temple)

8. What was he doing there? (Listening to the Jewish teachers and asking questions)

9. How long did his parents look for him? (Three days)

10. What did Jesus say he was doing? (He was about his Father's business)

11. Was Jesus an obedient son? (Yes)

12. What were the three ways Jesus grew? (In wisdom, stature, favor with God and man)

- Rebus Puzzle - "And the child grew and became strong in spirit." Luke 2:40

- Word Search Puzzle -

Lesson 5:

Review Questions:

1. Where was John the Baptist preaching? (Wilderness)

2. What was he preaching? (Repentance)

3. What prophet spoke about him being a "voice crying in the wilderness"? (Isaiah)

4. Describe John's clothing. (Camel's hair clothing and a leather belt)

5. What did John eat? (Locusts and wild honey)

6. Where did he baptize people? (Jordan River)

7. What two groups of people came to hear him and got a fiery sermon? (Pharisees and Sadducees)

8. What part of Jesus' clothing did John say he wasn't even worth to carry? (Sandals)

9. Where did Jesus travel from to come to John? (Galilee)

10. Why did Jesus want to be baptized? (To fulfill all righteousness, because it was right to do)

11. In what form did the Spirit of God descend upon Jesus? (Dove)

12. What did God say? ("This is my beloved Son in whom I am well pleased.")

- Crossword Puzzle -

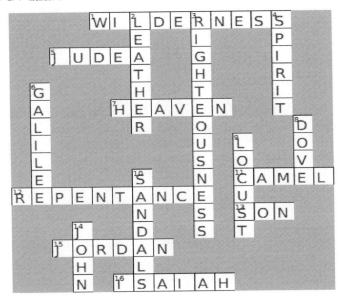

Lesson 6:

Review Questions:

1. Who led Jesus to the wilderness? (The Spirit of God)

2. How long did Jesus fast? (40 days and 40 nights)

3. Who came to tempt Jesus? (Satan)

4. What was the first temptation? ("If you're the Son of God, command these stones to be made into bread.")

5. How did Jesus respond? (He quoted scripture - "Man shall not live by bread alone but by every word that proceeds from the mouth of God.")

6. What was the second temptation? (Jesus was put on top of the temple and told if he was the Son of God, prove it by throwing himself down and seeing the angels come to His rescue.)

7. How did Jesus respond? (He quoted scripture - "You shall not tempt the Lord your God.")

8. What was the third temptation? (Jesus was taken to a high mountain and shown all the kingdoms of the world and told they'd all be his if he would worship Satan.)

9. How did Jesus respond? (He again used the word of God - "You shall worship the Lord your God and Him only shall you serve.")

10. Who came to minister to Jesus after the devil left him? (Angels)

11. What does John say are the three types of temptation? (Lust of the flesh, lust of the eye, and the pride of life)

*   Word Scramble – Jesus, tempted, devil, bread, temple, kingdoms, wilderness, fasted, stones, pinnacle, angels, worship

*   Scripture Matching – 1) Deuteronomy 8:3, 2) Matthew 5:8, 3) John 3:16, 4) Genesis 1:1, 5) Psalm 23:2, 6) Matthew 3:17, 7) Luke 2:52, 8) Luke 1:37, 9) Luke 2:11, 10) Deuteronomy 6:5

Lesson 7:

Review Questions:

1. What lake was Jesus standing by in Luke 5? (Gennesaret)

2. Whose boat did he get into? (Simon's)

3. How long had Simon Peter and his partners been fishing? (All night)

4. How much had they caught? (Nothing)

5. What happened when Jesus told them to cast their nets out again? (Their nets were full of fish)

6. What brothers were fishing partners of Simon Peter? (James and John)

7. Jesus said he would make the fishermen fishers of what? (Men)

8. What did Peter, James and John leave to follow Jesus? (All)

9. What is Levi's other name? (Matthew)

10. What was Levi's occupation? (Tax collector)

11. What did Levi leave behind to follow Jesus? (All)

12. Who was a disciple of John the Baptist who then followed Jesus? (Andrew)

13. What city was Philip from? (Bethsaida)

14. Whom did Philip go and tell about Jesus? (Nathanael)

15. Where did Jesus see Nathanael before Philip called him? (Under a fig tree)

16. What two things does Nathanael call Jesus? (Son of God, King of Israel)

- Guess the Disciple – 1) Matthew, 2) Andrew, 3) Philip, 4) Nathanael, 5) John, 6) James, 7) Peter, 8) Matthew, 9) Philip, 10) Peter, 11) Nathanael, 12) Andrew 13) James and John

- Word Search Puzzle -

Lesson 8:

Review Questions:

1. What city were Jesus and his disciples at? (Cana)

2. What event were they invited to? (A wedding)

3. What did they run out of at the feast? (Wine)

4. Who turned to Jesus for help? (His mother, Mary)

5. How many waterpots were there? (6)

6. About how many gallons did each waterpot hold? (20-30)

7. What were the pots made of? (Stone)

8. Whom did Jesus command the servants to give some wine to? (The master or ruler of the feast)

9. Whom did the master of the feast think had saved the best wine for last? (The bridegroom)

10. What did this first miracle of Jesus do? (Manifested his glory)

11. What city did Jesus travel to next? (Capernaum)

• Who Am I/What Am I? – 1) wedding, 2) waterpot, 3) bridegroom, 4) feast, 5) wine, 6) servant, 7) Jesus, 8) miracle, 9) disciples, 10) Mary

• Crossword Puzzle -

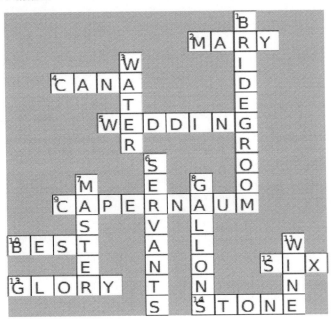

Lesson 9:

Review Questions:

1. What region did Jesus and his disciples travel to? (Samaria)

2. What city did they stop at? (Sychar)

3. What did Jesus sit down by? (Jacob's well)

4. What did the disciples go off to do? (Buy food)

5. What kind of water did Jesus talk about to the woman? (Living water)

6. How many husbands had the woman had? (5)

7. Was she currently married? (No)

8. What did the woman think Jesus was at first? (A prophet)

9. How did Jesus say people are to worship God? (In spirit and in truth)

10. What did Jesus admit to the woman? (That He was the Messiah)

11. What did the woman do when she found out who Jesus was? (Went into the city

and shared the good news with everyone)

12. What "harvest" was Jesus talking about? (Souls)

13. Did very many of the Samaritans believe? (Yes)

14. What did they all believe? (That Jesus was the Christ, the Savior of the world)

- Word Search Puzzle -

Lesson 10:

Review Questions:

1. Where did Jesus go to preach to the people? (On a mountain)

2. In the beatitudes, what will the merciful obtain? (Mercy)

3. What two things does Jesus compare our influence with? (Salt and light)

4. Is it okay to swear? (No)

5. What should we do for our enemies? (Love them, pray for them, do good to them)

6. Are we supposed to do good deeds so that everyone will notice and praise us? (No)

7. What does "hallowed" mean? (Holy)

8. If we aren't willing to forgive others, what will God not do for us? (Forgive us)

9. Where are we to lay up treasures? (In heaven)

10. Does Jesus want us to worry about what we'll eat or what we'll wear? (No)

11. Whom does God feed and clothe that are of less importance than we are? (The birds of the air and the flowers of the field)

12. What rich king was not dressed as beautifully as the lilies? (Solomon)

13. What will God give us if we seek Him first? (Those things we need)

14. What kind of gifts does God want to give us? (Good)

15. What does He want us to do first? (Ask)

16. What does the Golden Rule say? (Whatever you want men to do to you, do also to them or treat others the way you want to be treated)

17. How can we tell if someone is a false teacher? (By their fruits)

18. Whom does Jesus say will enter the kingdom of heaven? (Those who do the will of God or those who obey God)

19. Why did the wise man's house remain standing after the storm? (It was built on a rock)

20. How did the people react to the sermon of Jesus? (They were astonished)

- Sword Drill – 1) 5:9, 2) 7:1, 3) 6:11, 4) 6:19, 5) 5:16, 6) 7:12, 7) 6:9, 8) 5:41, 9) 6:33, 10) 7:7

- Matching – 1) for they shall see God, 2) of the earth, 3) before men, 4) your will be done, 5) who asks you, 6) how they grow, 7) all these things shall be added unto you, 8) do also to them, 9) that you be not judged, 10) you will know them

- Matching #2 – 1) Matthew 6:9, 2) Matthew 6:27, 3) Matthew 7:10, 4) Matthew 7:28, 5) Matthew 5:12, 6) Matthew 5:14, 7) Matthew 6:11, 8) Matthew 6:24, 9) Matthew 5:41, 10) Matthew 5:48

Lesson 11:

Review Questions:

1. What city did this likely take place in? (Capernaum)

2. Who was at the house with Jesus? (Pharisees and teachers of the law)

3. What was Jesus doing for the people? (Teaching and healing)

4. Why couldn't the paralyzed man get to Jesus? (The crowd was too big)

5. How did the paralytic's friends get him into the house? (They took him up to the roof, removed some tiles, and lowered his bed into the house before Jesus.)

6. What is the first thing Jesus said to him? ("Man, your sins are forgiven you.")

7. What did the scribes and Pharisees think Jesus was doing? (Blaspheming)

8. What did Jesus tell the paralytic to do? ("Arise, take up your bed, and go to your house.")

9. How long did it take the man to get up from his bed? (He arose immediately.)

10. What did he do as he went home? (Glorified God)

11. What did Jesus see that the paralytic and his friends had? (Faith)

12. What is the purpose of miracles? (To confirm the Word of God)

13. What was the crowd's reaction to this event? (They were amazed and glorified God.)

- Word Scramble – prayed, teaching, Pharisees, power, crowd, housetop, faith, blasphemies, hearts, arise, walk, strange

- Word Search Puzzle -

Lesson 12:

Review Questions:

1. What time of day did this occur? (Evening)

2. What is Jesus sitting in? (A boat)

3. What had he been doing all day? (Teaching the people)

4. Who was with him? (His disciples as well as other boats of people)

5. What arose? (A storm)

6. What was Jesus doing while this was going on? (Sleeping)

7. How did his disciples feel about that? (They were upset and thought he didn't care what they were going through.)

8. What did Jesus say to the wind and the waves? ("Peace be still")

9. What effect did this have on the weather? (The wind stopped and everything was calm)

10. What two things did Jesus ask them? (1. Why are you afraid? 2. Where is your faith?)

11. What was their reaction to his miracle? (They feared him and were amazed at him.)

12. What did they say obeyed Jesus? (The wind and the sea)

•   Crossword Puzzle -

Lesson 13:

Review Questions:

1. What was Jesus moved with when he saw the multitudes? (Compassion)

2. What kind of place were they in? (Deserted)

3. What did the people need because of the time of day? (Bread, or food)

4. What was the disciples' solution to the problem? (Send the people away to buy food in the villages)

5. What did Jesus tell the disciples to do? (Give them something to eat)

6. How much did the disciples think it was going to cost? (200 denarii)

7. Did the disciples have this amount? (No)

8. Who had some food to share? (A little boy)

9. How much food did he have? (Five loaves and two fish)

10. What did Jesus command everyone to do? (Sit down in groups)

11. What did Jesus do before he passed the food out to the people? (He prayed)

12. Did everyone get something to eat? (Yes)

13. How much food was leftover? (12 baskets full)

14. How many were fed by Jesus? (More than 5,000)

15. When the disciples got into their boat, where did Jesus go and why? (To a mountain to pray)

16. What difficulty did the disciples run into out in the middle of the sea? (Their boat was being tossed about in the waves because a strong wind had come up)

17. Jesus saw their difficulty and did what? (Walked on the water out to them)

18. What did the disciples think they were seeing? (A ghost)

19. What did Jesus say to them? (Be of good cheer! It is I; do not be afraid)

20. Who asked to come to Jesus on the water? (Peter)

21. What happened to him and why? (He started to sink because he took his eyes off Jesus)

22. What did Jesus do? (Reached out his hand and pulled him to safety)

23. What happened when Jesus got in the boat? (The wind ceased)

24. What did the disciples call Jesus? (The Son of God)

- Who Am I/What Am I? - 1) basket, 2) denarius, 3) little boy, 4) prayer, 5) crowd, 6) loaves, 7) Peter, 8) ghost, 9) wind, 10) boat

- Matching – 1) b, 2) h, 3) i, 4) e, 5) a, 6) j, 7) c, 8) f, 9) g, 10) d

Appendix A – Maps

Map 1 - Palestine

Map 2 – Egypt, Palestine, Mesopotamia

Map 3 – Sea of Galilee

Map 4 – Middle East, Far East, Africa

*Each map may be photocopied for personal home use as much as needed.

Map 1 - Palestine

Map 2 – Egypt, Palestine, Mesopotamia

(Map should be turned 90 degrees clockwise for proper orientation.)

Map 3 – Sea of Galilee

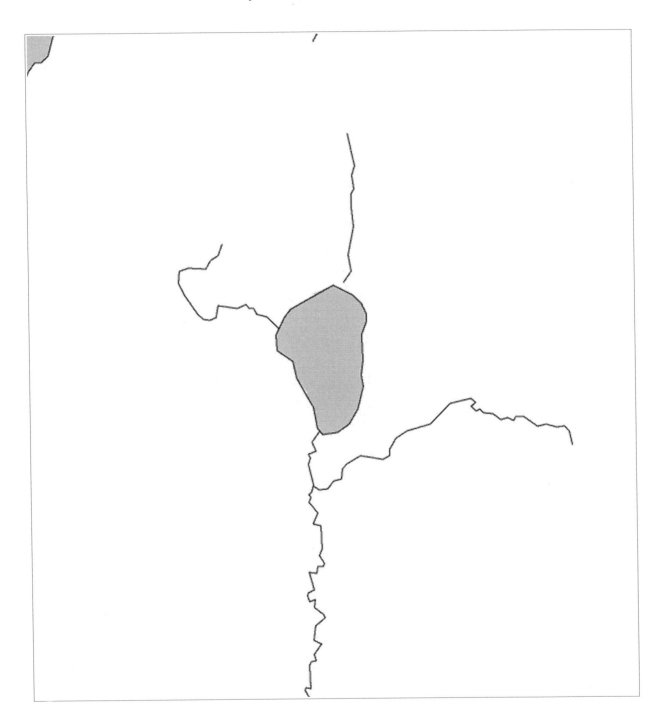

Map 4 – Middle East, Far East, Africa

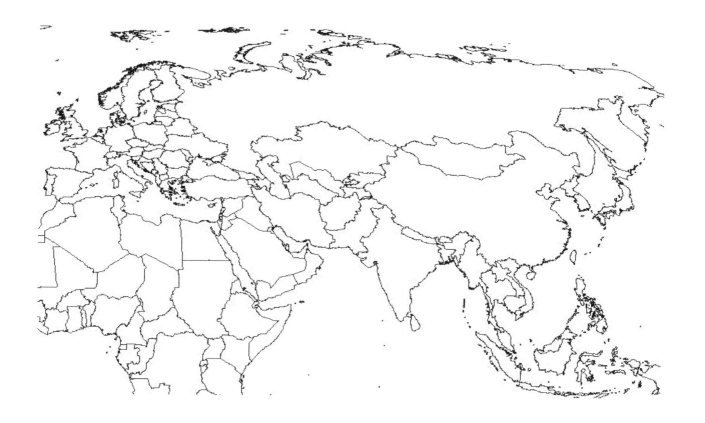

Appendix B – Templates

Lesson 3 – Star template

Lesson 7 – Fish template

Lesson 7 - Money bag template

Lesson 9 – Water droplets template

*Each item may be photocopied for personal home use as much as needed.

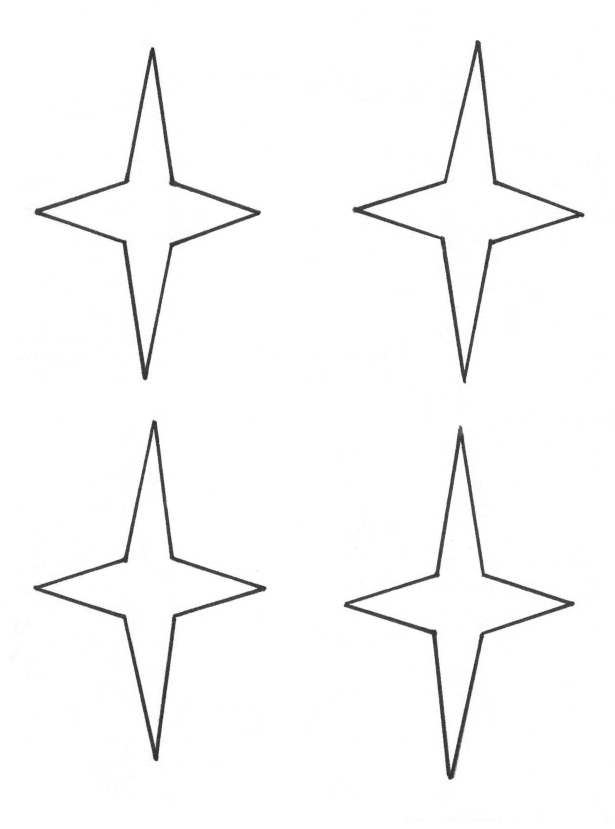

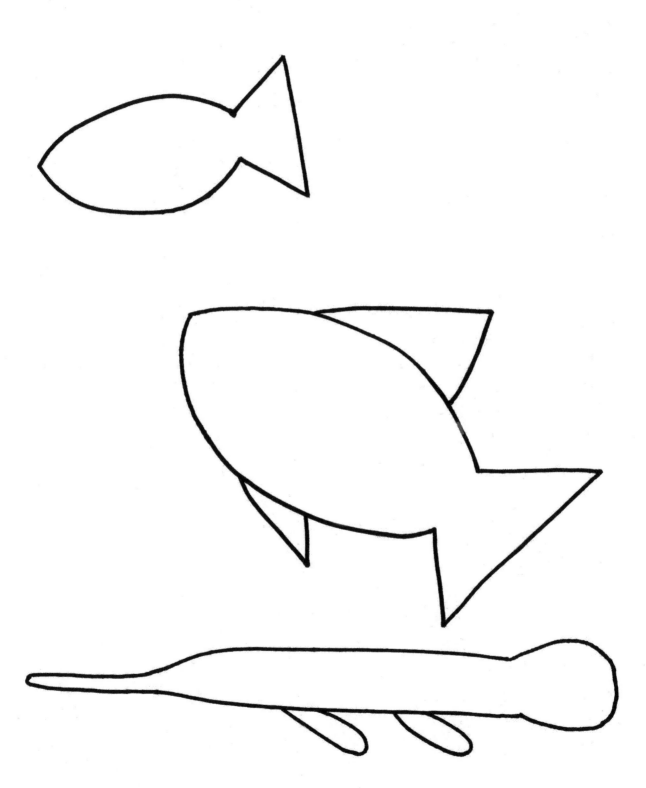

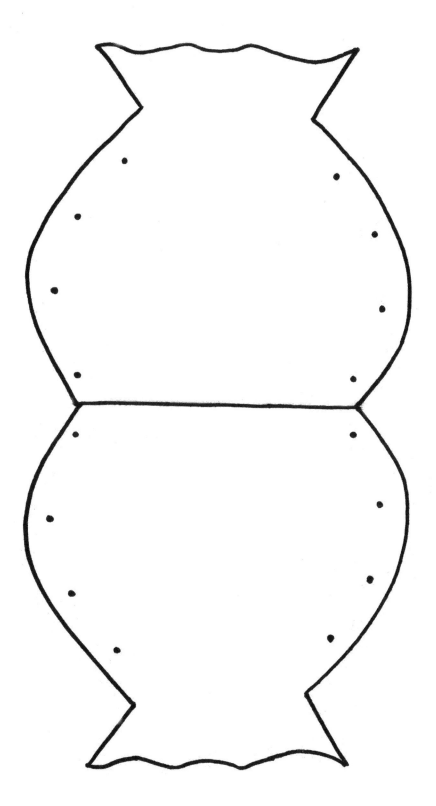

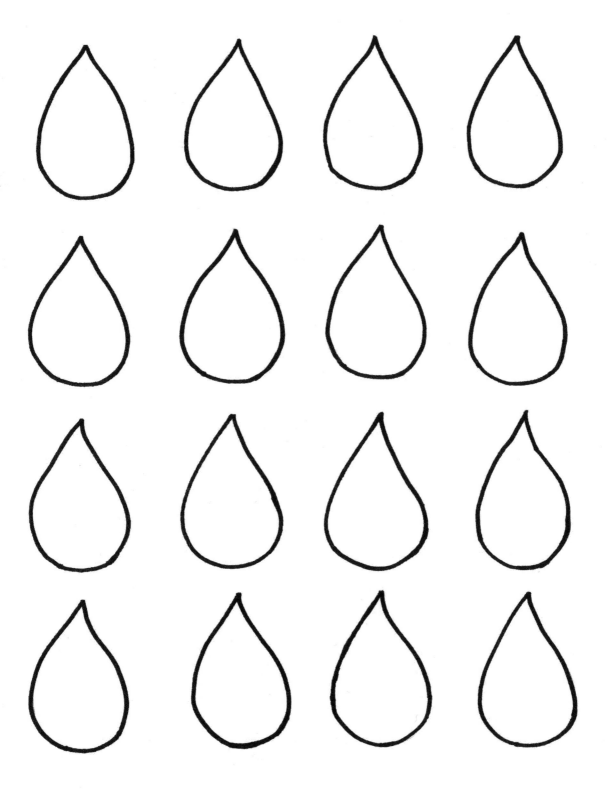

29724682R00066

Made in the USA
Charleston, SC
21 May 2014